Boom-Bust Cycles and
Financial Liberalization

Boom-Bust Cycles and Financial Liberalization

Aaron Tornell and
Frank Westermann

CESifo Book Series

The MIT Press
Cambridge, Massachusetts
London, England

MIT Press books may be purchased at special quantity discounts for business or sales promotional use. For information, please e-mail ⟨special_sales@mitpress.mit .edu⟩ or write to Special Sales Department, The MIT Press, 55 Hayward Street, Cambridge, MA 02142.

This book was set in Palatino on 3B2 by Asco Typesetters, Hong Kong.
Printed and bound in the United States of America.

Library of Congress Cataloging-in-Publication Data

Tornell, Aaron.
Boom-bust cycles and financial liberalization / Aaron Tornell and Frank Westermann.
    p.   cm.—(CESifo book series)
Includes bibliographical references and index.
ISBN 0-262-20159-3 (hc : alk. paper)
1. Finance—Developing countries. 2. Credit—Developing countries. 3. Financial crises—Developing countries. I. Westermann, Frank. II. Title. III. Series.
HG195.T67   2006
332'.09172'4—dc22   2005045104

10 9 8 7 6 5 4 3 2 1

To the memory of my mother, Lili, and my grandmother, Sheindl
—AT

To my wife, Tina, and my sons, Jannik and Tammo
—FW

Contents

Series Foreword

This volume is part of the CESifo Book Series. Each book in the series aims to cover a topical policy issue in economics. The monographs reflect the research agenda of the Ifo Institute for Economic Research, and they are typically "tandem projects," where internationally renowned economists from the CESifo network cooperate with Ifo researchers. The monographs have been anonymously refereed and revised after being presented and discussed at several workshops hosted by the Ifo Institute.

Acknowledgments

Many people have played key parts in the development of this book. We would like to thank our coauthors, Anne Krueger, Lorenza Martinez, Romain Ranciere, and Martin Schneider. Our understanding of boom-bust cycles has benefited from our academic interaction with them, and an important part of the contents in this book derives from our joint work with them.

We also would like to thank Helge Berger (former research director at CESifo) and Hans-Werner Sinn, who initiated this joint project. In addition, we thank CESifo for funding the project and hosting two workshops and for the hospitality of CES and UCLA that allowed us to work together.

Jay Dixon, Frank Denis Hiebsch, and Carolyn Sissoko provided excellent research assistance. Ulrich Hange and Silke Übelmesser did a great job handling the issues related to this book. Finally, special thanks are due to many people at MIT Press. In particular, we would like to thank our acquiring editor, Elizabeth Murry, and our production editor, Deborah Cantor-Adams.

Boom-Bust Cycles and
Financial Liberalization

1   Introduction

During the last two decades, many middle-income countries (MICs) have liberalized their financial markets. Such a policy has led to a greater incidence of crises, largely because liberalization has been associated with risky international bank flows and lending booms. As a result, several commentators have criticized financial liberalization, and have proposed that authorities intervene in financial markets to attain a slow-and-steady growth path.

Before following this policy recommendation restricting open and free capital markets, it is important to note the startling fact that over the last two decades, most of the fastest-growing countries of the developing world have experienced lending booms and busts. Countries in which credit growth has been smooth have, by contrast, exhibited the lowest growth rates.

It would thus appear that factors that contribute to financial fragility have also been a source of growth, even if they have led to greater fluctuations and even occasional crises. Therefore, to better understand economic fluctuations in MICs, it is necessary to determine what are the underlying distortions that affect financial markets in MICs, how their interaction makes fluctuations in MICs so large in magnitude relative to high-income countries (HICs), and why the forces that lead to greater growth also generate financial fragility. Such a conceptual framework allows one to make normative statements regarding liberalization policies.

The aim of this book is to address these points. Our approach to this task is divided into three parts. First, we characterize key macroeconomic regularities observed across MICs: we document the long-run link between liberalization, growth, and financial crises; we characterize patterns and comovements of key macroeconomic variables along the typical boom-bust cycle; we show that these comovements are observed more generally in tranquil times—that is, without conditioning on the occurrence of crises. We show that credit markets play a key role in such large fluctuations, not only in the boom-bust episodes that surround crises, but also in the strong "credit channel" observed during tranquil times—that is, in the strong response of the gross domestic product (GDP) and other macroeconomic variables to interest rate shocks.

In the second part of this book, we present a theoretical framework that explains how credit market imperfections prevalent in MICs can account for these empirical patterns. We then use this framework to address the normative question of whether financial liberalization is a good idea even if it leads to financial fragility. Lastly, in the third part, we provide microevidence on the credit market imperfections that drive the results of the theoretical framework. The synthesis presented in this book is based on joint papers we have written together and with Lorenza Martínez, Romain Ranciere, and Martin Schneider.

In comparison with HICs, the economic fluctuations experienced by MICs are of a much larger magnitude, and resemble more the Roaring Twenties and the Great Depression than the postwar business cycles of the Group of Seven (G7) countries. There is no evidence that MICs have systematically experienced more frequent and more severe exogenous shocks than HICs. What, then, can explain the severity of the boom-bust cycles, the strong credit channel, and the positive link between long-run growth and the incidence of crisis across MICs?

At the heart of the amplification mechanism is a sharp asymmetry between the tradables (T) sector and the more bank-dependent nontradables (N) sector. Each of the sectors reacts differently to shocks, with real exchange rate fluctuations playing a crucial role in amplification. While the N sector typically grows faster than the T sector during booms, it falls harder during crises and takes much longer to recover. Furthermore, this sectoral asymmetry is also observed during tranquil times: credit varies strongly with the N-to-T output ratio and movements in credit are strongly correlated with those of the real exchange rate—the relative price between N and T goods.

While this sectoral asymmetry has received little attention in the literature, it is key to understanding the patterns in MIC data. Throughout this book, the sharp responses of the N-to-T output ratio observed in the data will be derived from a sectoral asymmetry in financing opportunities prevalent in MICs: while T-sector firms tend to be large and have access to world capital markets, most N-sector firms are small and bank dependent. N-sector firms face severe contract enforceability problems and their lenders enjoy systemic bailout guarantees—that is, in the event of a crisis, lenders are bailed out at the taxpayers' expense.

We will argue that the mechanism that distinguishes the cyclic experience of MICs from that of HICs is based on the sectoral asymmetry in financing opportunities, differences in the degree of contract enforceability and the interaction of this imperfection with systemic bailout guarantees.

In a nutshell, the mechanism works as follows. Contract enforcement problems together with bailout guarantees generate stringent financing constraints and lead borrowers to take on credit risk, often in the form of currency mismatch. That is, debts are denominated in foreign currency, while the income streams that service those debts are in domestic currency. In such an economy, there is a strong balance sheet effect—that is, shocks to firms' cash flow have a strong effect on the economy. Moreover, fluctuation in the real exchange rate—that is, the relative price of T goods in terms of N goods—play a key amplifying role.

This "risky economy" exhibits a strong credit channel and can experience severe boom-bust cycles.

Despite the effects of financial fragility, in the long run, the risky economy outperforms the safe economy even in the presence of large crisis costs. This is because taking on credit risk permits constrained firms, most of which are in the N sector, to borrow and invest more during normal times, and because crises must be rare in order for agents to find it profitable to take on credit risk in the first place. As a result, the cumulative N-sector growth derived from higher investment in normal times outweighs the capital losses and the credit crunch experienced during a crisis. This translates into higher average GDP long-run growth because T-sector firms enjoy more abundant N-sector inputs.

Can one make the case for financial liberalization? Such a policy allows capital to flow more freely, and in addition it eliminates many regulatory barriers that prevent agents from taking on risk. This is why financial liberalization is typically followed by lending booms and then crises. Despite these crises, the lesson we should draw is not that financial liberalization is bad for growth and welfare. The analysis presented in this book shows that liberalization leads to higher growth because it eases financial constraints, but that this can occur only if agents take on credit risk. Therefore, high growth occurs at the cost of financial fragility.

A second, related point is that even though the entire economy must pay (through taxation) the crisis costs and the bailouts, everyone may gain from a risky credit path. Better access to capital benefits not only credit-constrained firms but the economy as a whole. For instance, an exporting firm that is not financially constrained will benefit from the fact that its suppliers have better financing opportunities and thus provide cheaper inputs. Hence, the whole economy can enjoy higher production efficiency.

An important policy lesson can be drawn from this discussion: Policies that try to reduce financial fragility may have the unintended consequence of choking off long-run growth. For example, a policy that blocks risky international bank flows, might starve many N-sector firms of external financing as foreign direct investment is directed mainly to the T sector. This, in turn, might generate bottlenecks for the T sector as N-sector inputs will stop growing.

We would like to stress that the arguments in this book depend on the existence of serious imperfections in the economic environment of MICs. We recognize that the first-best solution is to address the imperfections themselves—by improving contract enforcement and ending bailout guarantees. As a practical matter, however, it is not clear how to address either of these structural problems, and therefore we treat them as parameters of an MIC's economic environment. We do not intend to defend either corrupt practices— such as the granting of selective bailouts to politically connected agents—or unsustainable macroeconomic policies designed to delay unavoidable crises, but that lead to unnecessarily deep crises.

Models designed to study macroeconomic fluctuations in HICs are not directly applicable to MICs—in particular, because such models are not designed to account for the pronounced asymmetrical sectoral patterns, the sharp real exchange rate fluctuations, and the boom-bust cycles observed across MICs. Over the last decade, much research has been devoted to documenting the empirical regularities that distinguish MICs and developing models that account for such regularities.

The book is structured as follows. Chapter 2 presents a road map that connects the main points of the book. Chapter 3 examines the empirical link between liberalization, growth, and crises. Chapter 4 characterizes economic fluctuations in MICs. Chapter 5 contains the conceptual framework. Chapter 6 provides evidence on the credit market imperfections prevalent in MICs. And chapter 7 concludes with some policy implications.

2   Road Map

Here, we summarize the main points made in each of the subsequent chapters and discuss how these points connect with the main themes of the book that we have described in the introduction.

The first part of the book, chapters 3 and 4, is empirical. Chapter 3 concentrates on the long run, and establishes the link between liberalization, growth, and crises. Chapter 4 documents regularities observed at higher frequencies across MICs: the boom-bust patterns observed around crises as well as the strong credit channel observed during normal times.

Chapter 3 shows that across the set of countries with active financial markets, trade liberalization has typically been followed by financial liberalization. On average, both trade and financial liberalization have led to higher long-run per capita GDP growth. However, financial liberalization has led to financial fragility and occasional crises, furthermore, the positive link between growth and financial liberalization is not generated by a few high-growth countries that experienced no crisis. Rather, the countries that have experienced boom-bust episodes are typically the fastest-growing ones.

These facts do not contradict the negative link between growth and the *variance* of several macroeconomic variables—which is the typical measure of volatility in the literature. A high variance reflects not only the rare busts associated with occasional crises but also the occurrence of frequent ups and downs. Instead, we measure the incidence of occasional crises with the *negative skewness* of real credit growth. The findings show that fast-growing MICs tend to have negatively skewed credit growth paths.

To picture the macroeconomic trade-off between growth and macroeconomic risk observed across MICs, consider two examples: Thailand exhibits a steep but crisis-prone growth path, whereas India follows a slow but safe growth path. As we can see in figure 2.1, Thailand has experienced lending booms followed by crises, deep recessions, and credit crunches. Meanwhile, the growth of credit in India is slow but smooth. Our econometric estimates show that after controlling for the standard variables, Thailand has grown about 2 percent more per year than India during the period from 1980 to 2000. About a quarter of the growth differential between Thailand and India can be attributed to credit risk, as measured by the (negative) *skewness* of real credit growth.

The growth paths of liberalized MICs exhibit large fluctuations around trends that are remarkably similar across countries, despite differences in nominal exchange rate regimes. The analysis of such fluctuations will help us identify the mechanisms that link long-run economic growth and macroeconomic risk across MICs. This link, in turn, will help us understand why financial liberalization might be beneficial even if it makes economies prone to crises.

Chapter 4 characterizes the typical boom-bust cycle as well as the comovements and the strong credit channel observed in tranquil times. In contrast to earlier decades, large fiscal deficits have not been central to the new boom-bust cycles. Instead, bank lending has played a key role. Typically, following liberalization there is a lending boom and an appreciation of the real exchange rate. The boom eventually ends in twin crises during which a severe real depreciation coincides with a banking crisis and widespread default by domestic firms on unhedged foreign-currency-denominated debt.

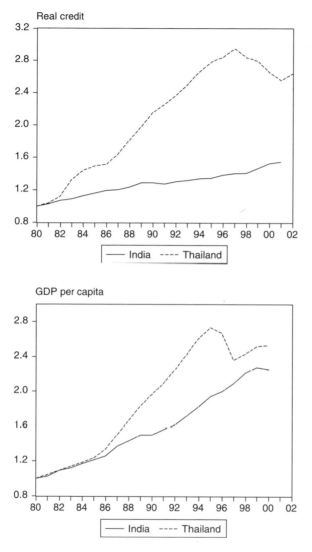

Figure 2.1
Safe versus risky growth paths

In the aftermath of the twin crises, there is typically a short-lived recession: GDP growth resumes a couple of years after the crisis. In contrast, credit growth stagnates and a protracted credit crunch develops long after aggregate GDP growth has resumed.

This puzzling coexistence of a credit crunch and GDP growth is closely related to the sharp *asymmetrical sectoral pattern* alluded to above: while the N sector typically grows faster than the T sector during a boom, it experiences a sharper fall during the crisis and takes longer to recover. This asymmetric sectoral response is critical to understanding the patterns in MIC data.

Another stylized fact that helps us restrict the class of models that can account for fluctuations in MICs is that investment is the component of GDP that experiences by far the largest swings over the cycle, and at the other extreme consumption varies the least.

The second part of chapter 4 shifts attention from what happens around crises and focuses instead on how credit market shocks are amplified during tranquil times. It shows that the strong comovements between credit, investment, the real exchange rate, and the ratio of N-to-T production also arise more generally without conditioning on the occurrence of crises (that is, during tranquil times). We then estimate vector autoregressions (VARs) using quarterly data for a group of countries and find that the so-called credit channel is strong in MICs. That is, shocks to the interest rate spread have a strong and statistically significant effect on GDP in MICs.[1] We also find that in response to an increase in the spread, there is a decline in credit growth, and the N-to-T output ratio as well as a real depreciation. This indicates that in MICs, sectoral asymmetries and real exchange rate fluctuations play a key role in amplification not only during crises but also during tranquil times.

Neither the strong credit channel nor the co-movements we have described are evident in HICs. To gain some perspective on the high amplitude of economic fluctuations in MICs, we compare Mexico and the United States. As we can see in figure 2.2, GDP in the United States has experienced small fluctuations around its trend. Mexico's GDP, in contrast, exhibits dramatic ups and downs. Furthermore, we can see that the behavior of key macrovariables around the 1991 U.S. recession is fundamentally different from that observed in Mexico around the 1994 crisis. It is evident that the United States has experienced neither pronounced asymmetrical sectoral patterns nor dramatic swings in the evolution of credit and the real exchange rate.[2] In contrast, Mexico exhibits dramatic boom-bust cycles typical of liberalized MICs.

In sum, the stylized facts documented in chapters 3 and 4 show that across MICs, liberalization has led to financial deepening and higher growth. This process, however, has not been smooth; it has been characterized by booms and busts, suggesting that the same mechanism that links liberalization with growth also generates large fluctuations and even occasional crises. Moreover, the evidence indicates that any successful theory of fluctuations in MICs must account for the pronounced asymmetrical sectoral patterns observed in these countries. Twin crises and MIC fluctuations in general are better understood as sectoral phenomena rather than aggregate phenomena. At *high frequencies*, asymmetrical sectoral patterns are necessary to explain not only the sharp fluctuations in the N-to-T output ratio alluded to above but also (1) the dramatic depreciations in the real exchange rate (the price of N goods relative to T goods) observed around crises, (2) the coexistence of fast GDP growth and credit crunches, and (3) the currency mismatch in balance sheets that pervades MICs. At *low frequencies*, asymmetrical sectoral patterns can help explain why countries that grow faster tend to experience crises.

During the last decade, several models have been developed to explain MIC fluctuations. In particular, to explain some aspects of the typical boom-bust cycle, "third-generation" crises models have looked to financial market imperfections as key fundamentals. The models are typically based on one of two distortions: either "bad

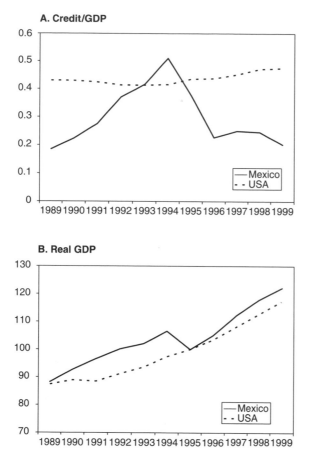

Figure 2.2
Mexico versus the United States

policy" in the form of bailout guarantees, or "bad markets" in the form of a credit market imperfection that induces balance sheet effects, such as asymmetrical information, or the imperfect enforceability of contracts. The first distortion leads to excessive risk taking, while the latter gives rise to borrowing constraints. In most of the literature, either borrowing constraints or credit risk arise in equilibrium, but not both. Clearly, to account for a boom-bust cycle it is necessary to have both. In general, though, the forces that

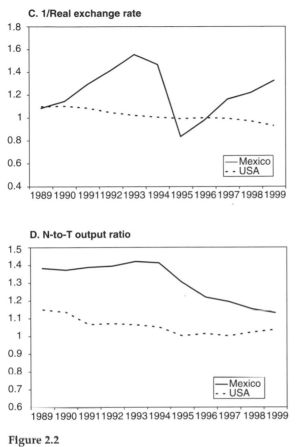

Figure 2.2
(continued)

generate endogenous credit risk, neutralize the forces that give rise to borrowing constraints. The first part of chapter 5 tackles this problem by using the model of Schneider and Tornell (2004), who consider an economy that is simultaneously subject to contract enforceability problems and systemic bailout guarantees, and show that their interaction gives rise to *both* borrowing constraints (lending is constrained by firms' cash flow) and credit risk (agents choose the "wrong" debt denomination, such as dollars instead of pesos, creating currency mismatch). Furthermore, the equilibrium path of such an economy generates a strong credit channel and delivers a dynamic explanation for a complete boom-bust episode without the need to assume exogenous real shocks.

As we mentioned earlier, asymmetrical sectoral patterns are key to understanding the patterns in MIC data. In the model presented in chapter 5, these patterns are derived from an asymmetry in financing opportunities between the T and N sectors prevalent in MICs: large firms, most of which are in the T sector, can finance themselves in international markets, while most firms in the N sector are financially constrained. The model captures this asymmetry by considering an economy where T-sector firms have access to perfect financial markets, while N-sector firms are run by managers who cannot commit to repay debt and thus face borrowing constraints.

Systemic bailout guarantees are the second main ingredient of the model. Guarantees induce agents to take on insolvency risk, which is crucial to generate self-fulfilling crises. It is a stylized fact that governments ensure creditors against systemic crises. That is, if a critical mass of borrowers is on the brink of bankruptcy, the government will implement policies to ensure that creditors get repaid (at least in part) and thus avoid an economic meltdown. These policies may come in the form of an easing of monetary policy, the maintenance of an exchange rate peg, or the handing out of checks.

How Do Borrowing Constraints and Currency Mismatches Arise?

It is well established in the literature that contract enforceability problems generate borrowing constraints because lenders impose lending ceilings proportional to the borrowers' net worth to ensure repayment. It is also well-known that bailout guarantees induce agents to take on insolvency risk because the downside risk is covered by the government. Combining both distortions is problematic because they act in opposite directions and in general neutralize each other. The contribution of Schneider and Tornell (2004), which we summarize in chapter 5, is to develop a setup where these opposing forces do not neutralize each other and a boom-bust cycle arises endogenously. Along the equilibrium path, there is a self-reinforcing mechanism that generates systemic credit risk. On the one hand, if N-sector firms expect the real exchange rate to fluctuate enough, they find it optimal to create a currency mismatch (by denominating their debt in T goods) and thereby risk going bankrupt in case of a drastic real depreciation. If all firms go bankrupt due to depreciation, this event triggers a bailout and shifts debt repayment to the taxpayer. Thus, the systemic bailout guarantee increases ex ante profits. On the other hand, since there is a currency mismatch, the balance sheet effect validates the initial expectation of real exchange rate fluctuations. This effect is due to the commitment problem generated by contract enforceability problems. Since the guarantees are systemic and do not ensure lenders against idiosyncratic default, an individual manager must respect a borrowing constraint to credibly abstain from stealing. As a result, N-sector investment is constrained by N-sector net worth.

Notice that in order for the argument to work, it is necessary that bailouts be systemic. If instead bailouts were granted unconditionally whenever there was an individual default, then the guarantees would neutralize the effects of contract enforceability problems and borrowing constraints would not arise in equilibrium. In other words institutions must be strong enough to withstand the political pressures to grant a bailout whenever an individual borrower defaults.

The Amplifying Mechanism

The interaction of borrowing constraints and currency mismatch gives rise to an amplifying mechanism that generates both a strong credit channel and (in an extreme case) self-fulfilling twin crises. To illustrate the amplifying mechanism, consider an equilibrium where N-sector agents face borrowing constraints and denominate their debt in foreign currency. In such an economy, a shift in expectations that increases the domestic interest rate implies that firms without access to international financial markets can now borrow less at each level of net worth. Lower borrowing results in lower investment. This direct effect is amplified because there is currency mismatch and part of the N sector's demand comes from the N sector itself. The fall in demand for N goods leads to further real depreciation. Since N-sector agents have dollar debt on the books, while their revenues are denominated in local currency, there is a fall in the N sector's profits and net worth. A vicious cycle ensues as lower net worth leads to even lower investment, which leads to a lower demand for N goods and a steeper real depreciation, which leads to lower net worth and so on. This is the *balance sheet effect* that acts as a financial accelerator to amplify the effect of shocks on the economy.

To see why the comovements we alluded to above arise in equilibrium, notice that T-sector agents have access to international capital markets and can more easily substitute away from domestic borrowing. Thus, their decisions are mostly affected by the world interest rate, not by the domestic lending rate. An increase in the spread between these two interest rates is therefore associated with a real depreciation, a decline in the N-to-T output ratio, and a fall in credit. Furthermore, the sectoral asymmetry implies that the decline in GDP growth is milder than that of credit. This explains the persistent swings in the credit-to-GDP ratio observed in the data.

The Boom-Bust Cycle

To see how the model can generate a complete boom-bust cycle notice that under some circumstances, the vicious cycle we have described can generate a sufficiently large depreciation that bankrupts N-sector agents with T debt on their books. In this case, a self-fulfilling crisis occurs. As in the data, crises in the model are preceded by a real appreciation as well as a lending boom. The boom features high leverage and risk taking in the form of currency mismatch by firms in the N sector. As a result, the economy becomes vulnerable to a self-fulfilling depreciation. In the aftermath of a crisis, the wealth of the N sector collapses. This generates a credit crunch that affects mainly the N sector. T-sector agents, on the other hand, do not face a decline in demand and have access to international financial markets. As a result, T output is not negatively affected and so the N-to-T output ratio falls as observed in the data.

We stress that exogenous real shocks are not necessary to generate crises. A shift in expectations regarding the likelihood of a bailout is sufficient. Moreover, the mechanism at work is independent of the nominal exchange rate regime. This is an attractive property as countries with both fixed and floating exchange rates have experienced boom-bust cycles.

Liberalization and Growth

The second part of chapter 5 embeds the credit market game we have described into an endogenous growth model in order to generate a growth path in which boom-bust cycles develop. This part of the book, which is based on the work of Ranciere, Tornell, and Westermann (2003), establishes a causal link from liberalization to growth, and shows how, in the presence of severe credit market imperfections, the forces that lead to higher growth also generate financial fragility.

Consider the two-sector economy we described above, where N goods are used as inputs in both the N and T sectors, and where N-sector agents face severe contract enforceability problems. Suppose that liberalization has not taken place, so that N-sector agents cannot take on credit risk and must denominate their debt in N goods. In such an economy, the N sector will face stringent borrowing constraints and exhibit a low investment rate. Since N goods serve as intermediate inputs for both sectors, the retarded N-sector growth constrains the long-run growth of the T sector and GDP: there is a *"bottleneck."*

In such an economy, trade liberalization increases GDP growth by promoting T-sector productivity. Financial liberalization adds even more to GDP growth by accelerating financial deepening and thus increasing the investment of financially constrained N-sector firms. This occurs because financial liberalization lifts restrictions that prevent risk taking. Yet as we have seen, the easing of borrowing constraints is associated with the undertaking of credit risk, which, in the model, takes the form of foreign currency—denominated debt backed by N output.

The easing of borrowing constraints allows N-sector firms to invest more. High N-sector growth, in turn, helps the T sector grow faster by providing abundant and cheap inputs. As long as a crisis does not occur, growth in a liberalized risky economy is greater than in a nonliberalized safe one. Of course, financial fragility implies that a self-fulfilling crisis may occur. And during crises, GDP growth falls. A key point is that crises must be rare in order to occur in equilibrium—otherwise agents would not find it profitable to take on credit risk in the first place. Hence, average long-run growth is greater along a risky path than along a safe one even if there are large crisis costs.

The Case for Financial Liberalization

In the third part of chapter 5, we sketch the argument used by Ranciere, Tornell, and Westermann (2003) to establish conditions under which the welfare costs of crises are outweighed by the benefits of higher growth generated by financial liberalization.

Because both sectors compete every period for the available supply of N goods, when contract enforceability problems are severe,
the N sector attains low leverage and commands only a small share
of N inputs for reinvestment. This results in a socially inefficient
low-growth path: a central planner would increase the N-sector
investment share to attain the Pareto optimal allocation. Clearly,
the first best allocation can be attained in a decentralized economy
by reducing the agency problems that generate the financing constraints. If such a reform is not feasible, however, financial liberalization may be a second-best instrument to increase social welfare
despite the side effect of financial fragility.

Ranciere, Tornell, and Westermann (2003) show that when contract enforceability problems are severe, but not too severe, and crisis costs are not excessively large, credit risk increases social welfare
and brings the allocation nearer to the Pareto optimal level. Furthermore, T-sector agents might even find it profitable to fund the fiscal
cost of the guarantees. The funding of the guarantees actually effects
a redistribution from the nonconstrained T sector to the constrained
N sector. This redistribution is to the mutual benefit of both sectors.
These results imply that in the presence of severe credit market
imperfections, financial liberalization is welfare improving *only if*
it leads to financial fragility, which makes the economy prone to
booms and busts. Clearly, these results do not imply that liberalization can attain the first best. The latter is attained by eliminating the
enforceability problems—which generate borrowing constraints—
through the implementation of judicial reform. Puzzlingly, most of
the countries that have liberalized trade and finance during the last
two decades have not reformed their judicial system.

Evidence for the Credit Market Imperfections

Chapter 6 documents three credit market imperfections that
are prevalent in MICs and underlie the mechanism we consider

throughout the book: asymmetrical sectoral financing opportunities, currency mismatch, and systemic bailout guarantees. This chapter is based on Tornell and Westermann (2003) and Tornell, Westermann, and Martínez (2003), which use three microlevel data sets: the *World Business Economic Survey* of the World Bank, the Mexican economic census, and the firms listed on the Mexican stock exchange.

Policy Implications

In the last chapter, we present several policy lessons that can be derived from the analysis in this book. Here, we list three of them. First, trade and financial liberalization will not, by themselves, solve the structural problem of a country. In particular, they must be complemented by judicial reform to improve the enforceability of contracts. Second, in the absence of judicial reform, there is a trade-off between growth and macroeconomic stability. Policies that preclude credit risk taking may have the unintended consequence of choking off long-run growth. Third, trying to delay an inevitable crisis may simply exacerbate the costs of the crisis. It is more important to concentrate on how to respond to the crisis. Specifically, GDP growth typically resumes fast in the aftermath of a crisis. Yet hoping that fast GDP growth will solve the nonperforming loans problem is wishful thinking. Because of the asymmetrical sectoral financing opportunities we have emphasized, GDP growth masks a decaying N sector that underlies the deteriorating banking system. This unbalanced path is unsustainable over the long run, as the experience of several countries has shown.

3   The Long Run: Liberalization, Growth, and Crises

In this chapter, we analyze empirically the links among liberalization, financial fragility, and growth across the set of countries with functioning financial markets. Several observers have indicated that liberalization might not be growth enhancing because it leads to crises. To address this point, we will show that trade liberalization is typically followed by financial liberalization—a process that does indeed lead to booms and busts—yet we will also show that financial fragility has been associated with faster GDP growth in spite of the fact that it leads to crises. Clearly, liberalization without fragility is best, but the data suggest that this combination is not available to MICs.[1]

In chapter 5, we will present a model that explains why, in the presence of severe credit market imperfections, liberalization leads to higher growth by easing financial constraints, but also induces financial fragility as a by-product. Because financial liberalization generates both financial deepening and crises, any analysis of the effects of financial liberalization must weigh the benefits of liberalization against its costs. In short, it would be a mistake to reject financial liberalization by focusing only on its costs and its tendency to lead to crises. An occasional crisis thus may be a price worth paying for faster growth.

The mechanism we have described in the previous chapter operates only in countries having a basic level of contract enforcement that permits agents to attain high enough leverage to reap the benefits of liberalization. Given this, we restrict our data set to countries where the ratio of stock market turnover to GDP was greater than 1 percent in 1998. This set consists of sixty-six countries, fifty-two of which have data available for the period 1980–1999. We will partition this set into seventeen HICs and thirty-five MICs.[2]

To assess the effects of liberalization, we analyze several macroeconomic variables before and after dates of liberalization. To do this, we construct two de facto indexes that signal the year during which an MIC switches from closed to open. The trade liberalization index signals that a country is open if its ratio of trade (exports plus imports) to GDP exhibits a trend break or is greater than 30 percent. The financial liberalization index signals an opening when the series of cumulative capital inflows experiences a trend break or if they exceed 10 percent of GDP. The idea is that a large change in a measure of openness indicates that a policy reform has taken place and that the reform has had a significant effect on actual flows.

As explained in more detail in the appendix, we identify the break points using the cumulative sum of residuals (CUSUM) method. The opening dates identified by our indexes are, in most cases, similar to those identified by the stock market liberalization index of Bekaert, Harvey, and Lundblad (2001), the financial liberalization index of Kaminsky and Schmukler (2002), and the trade liberalization index of Sachs and Warner (1997).[3]

The country years identified as liberalized by our indexes do not always coincide with good economic times, during which capital is flowing in and the economy is booming. Liberalized country years include both boom and bust episodes.

All the HICs in our sample have been open since 1980, which is the beginning of our sample period. Figure 3.1 exhibits the shares of MICs in our sample that have become open to trade and financial flows. It shows that in 1980, only 25 percent of these countries were

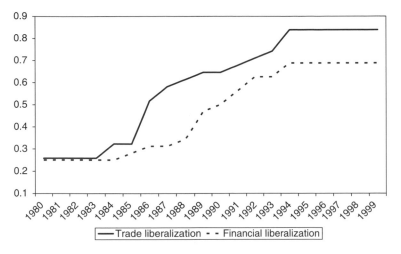

Figure 3.1
Share of countries that liberalized trade and financial flows
Note: The figure shows the share of countries that have liberalized relative to the
total number of MICs in our sample.
Source: Our own calculations.

open to trade. Most of these countries started to liberalize in the
mid-1980s, and 84 percent had liberalized their trade by 1999.

Several observers have suggested that to avoid volatility, countries should liberalize trade but not financial flows. Our first stylized fact indicates that this has typically not occurred.

Stylized Fact 3.1 *Over the last two decades, trade liberalization has
typically been followed by financial liberalization.*

Our indexes show that by 1999, 72 percent of countries that had liberalized trade had also liberalized financial flows, bringing the share
of MICs that are financially liberalized from 25 percent in 1980 to
69 percent. This close association suggests that an open trade regime is usually sustained with an open financial regime because
exporters and importers need access to international financial markets. Since capital is fungible, it is difficult to insulate the financial

flows associated with trade transactions. A few exceptions, such as India, Sri Lanka, and Venezuela, have liberalized trade but have not liberalized their financial markets.

The hypothesis that trade liberalization leads to financial liberalization can be tested with Granger causality tests. The null hypothesis that trade liberalization does not lead to financial liberalization is rejected, with an F-statistic of 3.671,[4] which corresponds to a p-value of 0.05. By contrast, the null hypothesis that financial liberalization does not lead to trade liberalization cannot be rejected, with an F-statistic of only 0.018, which corresponds to a p-value of 0.98.

Liberalization and GDP Growth

In this section, we show that across the set of countries with functioning financial markets, both trade and financial liberalization have been, on average, good for growth. This result confirms similar links established in the literature. Later on, we address the point mentioned at the beginning of this chapter that liberalization might not be growth enhancing because it leads to crises. We will show that, indeed, financial liberalization has typically been followed by booms and busts, but also that financial fragility has been associated with faster GDP growth in spite of the fact that it leads to crises.

In this chapter, we will not say anything about causality. Chapter 5 presents a model that shows that in the presence of credit market imperfections, liberalization leads to faster growth because it allows financially constrained firms to undertake credit risk, which both eases borrowing constraints and generates financial fragility, thus leading to occasional crises. The model establishes a causal link from liberalization to growth and has testable implications, which we will use to identify the mechanism.

Figure 3.2 shows that financial liberalization is associated with faster GDP growth. The figure depicts GDP growth rates in MICs

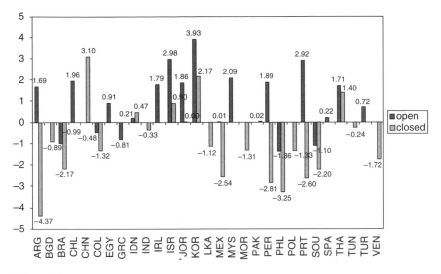

Figure 3.2
Liberalization and growth
Notes: The country episodes are constructed using windows of different lengths for each country. Country episodes that are shorter than five years are excluded. Averaging over these periods, we estimate a simple growth regression by ordinary least squares (OLS) in which real per capita growth is the dependent variable, and that only includes the respective initial income and population growth. The figure plots the residuals from this regression.

before and after financial liberalization, after controlling for initial income per capita and population growth.[5] This simple graphic representation reveals two patterns. First, growth is on average more rapid in open-country episodes than in closed ones.[6] Second, in almost every country the open episode exhibits more rapid growth than the closed episode.[7]

In order to assess the link between liberalization and growth, we add our liberalization variables to a standard growth regression:

$$\Delta y_{it} = \lambda y_{i,\text{ini}} + \gamma X_{it} + \phi_1 TL_{it} + \phi_2 FL_{it} + \varepsilon_{jt}, \tag{3.1}$$

where Δy_{it} is the average growth rate of the GDP per capita; $y_{i,\text{ini}}$ is the initial level of the GDP per capita; X_{it} is a vector of control

variables that includes initial human capital, the average population growth rate, and life expectancy; and TL_{it} and FL_{it} are our trade
and financial liberalization indicators, respectively. We do not include investment among the control variables because we expect
trade and financial liberalization to affect GDP growth through
higher investment.

We estimate the regression in three different ways. First, we estimate a standard cross-sectional regression by ordinary least squares
(OLS). In this case, 1980 is the initial year. TL_{it} and FL_{it} take values
between 0 and 1, specifying the share of years that the country was
liberalized during our sample period $[0, 0.05, 0.1, \ldots, 1]$. Second, we
estimate a panel regression using two nonoverlapping windows of
time: 1980–1989 and 1990–1999. Here, the liberalization variables
again take a value between 0 and 1 during each subperiod. Finally,
we use overlapping time windows. For each country and variable,
we construct ten-year averages starting with the period 1980–1989
and rolling forward to the period 1990–1999. Each country thus has
up to ten data points in the time-series dimension. In this case, the
liberalization variables take values in the interval $[0, 1]$, depending
on the proportion of liberalized years in a given window. We estimate the panel regressions using generalized least squares (GLS).
We deal with the resulting autocorrelation in the residuals by
adjusting the standard errors according to the method developed
by Newey and West (1987).[8]

Table 3.1 reports the estimation results. The financial liberalization variable enters significantly at the 5 percent level in all regressions in which it appears. The cross-sectional regression (column 1)
shows that following financial liberalization, growth in the GDP per
capita increases by 2.4 percentage points a year, after controlling for
the standard variables. The corresponding estimates are 1.7 percentage points in the nonoverlapping panel regression (column 2) and
2.5 percentage points in the overlapping windows regression (column 3). The last regression is similar to those estimated by Bekaert,

Harvey, and Lundblad (2001) using stock market liberalization dates. They find that GDP growth increases in the range of 0.4 to 1.5 percentage points.

Column 4 in panel A of table 3.1 shows that following trade liberalization, GDP growth increases 1.8 percentage points a year. This estimate is similar to the 2 percentage point increase found by Sachs and Warner (1997). Notice that the increase in GDP growth is greater following financial liberalization than following trade liberalization. Moreover, column 5 shows that when we include both variables in the growth regression, the marginal effect of trade liberalization falls to 1.6 percentage points, whereas that of financial liberalization increases (to 2.8 percentage points). The larger effect of financial liberalization suggests that in addition to the productivity gains from trade liberalization, the easing of financial constraints has been an important source of growth. The effect of financial liberalization will be the focus of the model we present below. Finally, column 6 shows that the positive link between liberalization and growth is also evident in the larger sample that includes HICs as well as MICs.

To deal with the possible endogeneity of the liberalization variables, panel B of table 3.1 reports estimation results from two-stage least squares (2SLS) regressions using as instruments the legal origin index of La Porta, Lopez de Silanes, and Zamarripa (2002) (column 7) as well as lagged values of all the variables in the regression (column 8). The table also reports results of regressions with fixed effects (column 9), and regressions excluding China and Ireland (columns 10 and 11), which may be driven by other factors. Our benchmark results in the first three columns are robust to these different estimation methods. The following stylized fact summarizes our findings.

Stylized Fact 3.2 *Over the period 1980–1999, both trade liberalization and financial liberalization are associated with more rapid growth in*

Table 3.1
Growth in the GDP per capita with trade and financial liberalization

Independent variable	1[a]	2[b]	3[c]	4[c]	5[c]	6[d]
Panel A: Main regressions						
Financial liberalization	2.363** (0.533)	1.691** (0.603)	2.502** (0.101)		2.777** (0.115)	2.278** (0.172)
Trade liberalization				1.784** (0.155)	1.606** (0.105)	0.147** (0.021)
Summary statistics						
Adjusted R^{2e}	0.546	0.633	0.692	0.544	0.747	0.802
Number of observations	34	59	290	300	280	440

	7[f]	8[g]	9[h]	10[i]	11[j]
Panel B: Robustness					
Financial	2.980** (0.363)	3.036** (0.668)	1.571** (0.181)	2.686** (0.132)	2.467** (0.119)
Trade				1.784** (0.155)	1.606** (0.105)
Summary					
Adjusted R^{2e}	0.615	0.615	0.953	0.547	0.568
Number of observations	423	423	460	450	450

Notes: The estimated equation is equation (3.1) in the text; the dependent variable is the average annual growth rate of the real GDP per capita. Control variables include initial per capita income, secondary schooling, population growth, and life expectancy. Standard errors are reported in parentheses and are adjusted for heteroskedasticity according to Newey and West (1987).

a. Standard cross-sectional regression estimated by OLS for the period 1980–1999.

b. Nonoverlapping panel regression estimated by GLS with two periods, 1980–1989 and 1990–1999.

c. Overlapping panel regression estimated by GLS with data as ten-year averages starting with 1980–1989 and rolling forward to 1990–1999.

d. Same as column 5, but with the addition of high-enforceability countries.

e. The adjusted R^2 is likely to overestimate the share of the variance explained by our right-hand-side variables because of the overlapping nature of the regression. For adjusting the R^2, no method comparable to that of Newey and West for the standard errors exists, and therefore the values need to be interpreted carefully.

f. Same as column 3, but using the legal origin index of La Porta, Lopez de Silanes, and Zamarripa (2002) as instruments in a 2SLS regression.

g. Same as column 3, but using lagged values as instruments in a 2SLS regression.

h. Same as column 3, but including fixed effects.

i. Same as column 3, but excluding China.

j. Same as column 3, but excluding Ireland.

**Significant at the 5 percent level.

the GDP per capita across the set of countries with functioning financial markets.

The existing literature provides mixed evidence on whether openness promotes long-run growth.[9] This can be attributed either to the indicators of openness used or the sample considered. We find a statistically significant link for two reasons. First, we identify liberalization *dates* that allow us to compare performance during liberalized country years with that during nonliberalized ones. Second, we restrict our analysis to the set of countries that have functioning financial markets because only in these countries do we expect our mechanism to work.

In contrast, many papers that do not find a significant link use de jure liberalization indexes or de facto indexes that do not identify liberalization dates. Yet the de jure indexes currently available for a large set of countries do not accurately reflect countries' de facto access to international financial markets. A country that has liberalized de jure may not implement the new policy for many years or may simply lack access to international financial markets despite having liberalized. For example, some African countries are de jure more financially liberalized than most Latin American ones yet have much smaller international financial flows. Several de facto "openness indexes" measure the size of some capital flow categories over the sample period. But because these openness indexes do not identify a specific year of liberalization, they are not appropriate for comparing the behavior of macroeconomic variables before and after liberalization.

Liberalization, Lending Booms, and Financial Fragility

Financial liberalization has often been criticized on the grounds that it leads to crises, which are bad for growth. This argument is neither empirically nor conceptually correct; that financial liberalization leads to infrequent crises does not mean that financial liberalization is bad for growth over the long run. We will show that financial liberalization does indeed lead to a greater incidence of crisis. Then we will demonstrate that the average positive link between liberalization and growth documented above *is not* driven by those rapid-growth countries that have had no crises. Instead, countries that grow faster tend to have crises. That is, there is a strong statistical link between the incidence of crises and long-run growth. This finding does not imply that crises are good for (or cause) growth.

The model we present in chapter 5 will show that in the presence of severe credit market imperfections, the forces that generate financial deepening and growth also generate—as a by-product—financial fragility. Because financial liberalization generates both financial deepening and crises, any analysis of the effects of financial liberalization must weigh its benefits against its costs. In short, it would be a mistake to reject financial liberalization by focusing only on its costs and its tendency to lead to crises.

To address systematically the issues discussed above, we need a measure of financial fragility. Unfortunately, no existing indexes of financial fragility are comparable across countries. In keeping with the spirit of this book, we use instead a de facto measure of fragility: negative skewness of credit growth. That is, we capture the existence of fragility by one of its symptoms: infrequent, sharp, and abrupt falls in credit growth. These abrupt falls occur during the banking crises that are characteristic of the boom-bust cycles that typically follow financial liberalization. During the boom, bank credit expands rapidly and excessive credit risk is undertaken. As a result, the economy becomes financially fragile and prone to crisis. Although the likelihood that a lending boom will crash in a given year is low, many lending booms do eventually end in a crisis.[10] During such a crisis, new credit falls abruptly and recuperates only gradually.

It follows that a country that experiences a boom-bust cycle exhibits rapid credit growth during the boom, a sharp and abrupt fall during the crisis, and slow credit growth during the credit crunch that develops in the wake of the crisis. Since credit does not jump during the boom and crises happen only occasionally, in financially fragile countries the distribution of credit growth rates is characterized by negative outliers. In statistical terms, countries that experience boom-bust cycles exhibit a *negatively skewed* distribution of credit growth. In plain language, the path of credit growth is "bumpy."[11]

If we had infinite data series, the negative skewness of credit growth would be an ideal measure of financial fragility. But in a finite sample, the index may overlook some cases of fragility that do not—yet—reflect bumpiness. Because most MICs that have followed risky credit paths experienced at least one major crisis during our sample period (1980–1999), we find that negative skewness of credit growth is a good indicator of the riskiness of the credit path followed by a given country.

Figure 3.3 depicts the kernel distributions of credit growth rates for India, Mexico, and Thailand.[12] Credit growth in India, a typical example of a nonliberalized country, has a low mean, and the data are quite tightly distributed around the mean, with skewness close to zero. Meanwhile, credit growth in Thailand, a prime example of a liberalized economy, has an asymmetrical distribution and is characterized by negative skewness. Mexico, like Thailand, has an asymmetrical distribution and its mean is closer to that of Thailand than to that of India.

Table 3.2 shows that the link between financial liberalization and bumpiness holds more generally across MICs. The table partitions country years into two groups: years before financial liberalization and years after. The table shows that financial liberalization leads to an increase in the mean of credit growth of 4 percentage points

A. Kernel densities

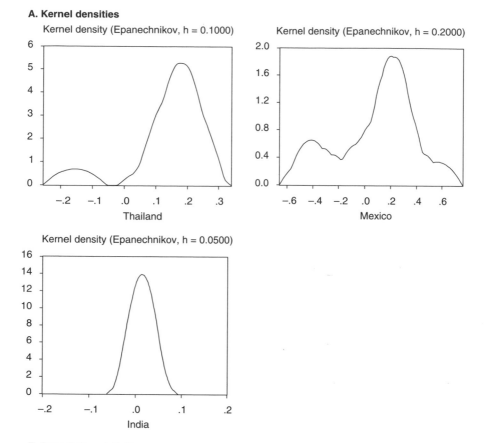

B. Descriptive statistics

	Thailand	Mexico	India
Mean	0.143	0.091	0.014
Standard deviation	0.110	0.303	0.014
Skewness	−1.945	−0.537	0.157

Figure 3.3

Credit growth distributions

Note: The sample period is 1988–1999. The kernel density function is a weighting function that determines the shape of the distribution. The Epanechnikov kernel estimator is given by $(3/4)(1 - u^2)I$ ($|u| \leq 1$), where u is the argument of the kernel function and I is an indicator variable that takes a value of one if the argument is true, and zero otherwise.

Table 3.2
Moments of credit growth before and after financial liberalization

	Liberalized country years	Nonliberalized country years
MICs		
Mean	0.078	0.038
Standard deviation	0.151	0.170
Skewness	−1.086	0.165
HICs		
Mean	0.025	NA
Standard deviation	0.045	NA
Skewness	0.497	NA

Notes: The table partitions the sample in two country year groups: liberalized and nonliberalized. The table compares the moments of credit growth across these two groups. Before the computations of the standard deviation and skewness, the means were removed from the series. We also corrected for data mistakes in New Zealand, Great Britain, and Belgium.

(from 3.8 to 7.8 percent) and a fall in the skewness of credit growth from near 0 to −1.08, and has only a negligible effect on the variance of credit growth. This illustrates the following stylized fact.

Stylized Fact 3.3 *Across MICs, financial liberalization has been followed by financial deepening. This process, however, has not been smooth; it is characterized by booms and occasional busts.*

Notice that, across HICs, credit growth exhibits near 0 skewness, and both the mean and the variance are smaller than across MICs. As we will argue below, this difference reflects the absence of severe credit market imperfections in HICs.

The effect of financial liberalization on the mean and the bumpiness of credit growth is represented visually in the event study in figure 3.4. The top panel shows the deviation of the credit-to-GDP ratio, after liberalization, from its mean in normal times (that is, the

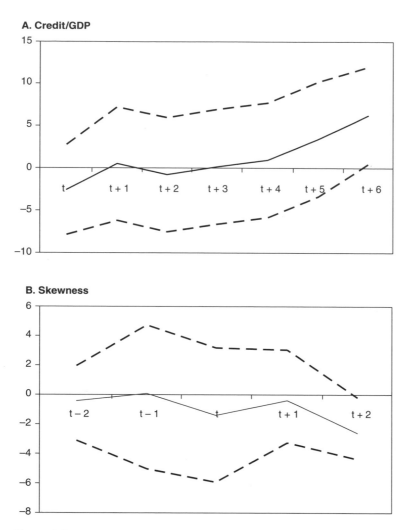

Figure 3.4
Financial liberalization, lending booms, and bumpiness
Notes: In panel B, "skewness" refers to the skewness of real credit growth during the following ten years. The event windows were constructed from panel regressions of the respective variable on dummy variables that take a value of one in the period where a country liberalized, and zero otherwise. The panel regressions are estimated with fixed effects, using a GLS estimator.
Source: Authors' calculations.

years not covered by the dummy variables in the regression). Over the six years following the liberalization date, the credit-to-GDP ratio increases on average by 6 percentage points, and this cumulative increase is significant at the 5 percent level. The bottom panel shows the increase in negative skewness, which reflects the increase in bumpiness.[13] Here, the average negative skewness increases from about 0 to -2.5, which is also significant at the 5 percent level.

Are Crises Rare?

Two conditions are key to our contention that financial liberalization is growth enhancing even if it makes the economy prone to crises: that a crisis be preceded by a lending boom, and that crises be rare events. If the latter condition did not hold, and the undertaking of credit risk led to frequent crises, then credit growth would not exhibit negative skewness but rather higher variance, and GDP growth would be lower than along a safe path. Furthermore, as the model below shows, crises must be rare in order for them to occur in equilibrium; agents will be unwilling to take on credit risk if the probability of bankruptcy is not small enough to begin with.

To investigate whether these two conditions are satisfied in our sample, we compute conditional probabilities of crises and booms. Our estimates in table 3.3 correspond to the case in which a lending boom is a pair of country years in which credit experiences a cumulative growth of more than 20 percent (30 or 40 percent). The first column shows that crises tend to be preceded by booms: $p(lb|cr) =$ 86 percent. The converse is not true, though: If a boom starts at t, the probability of a crisis in either $t+2$ or $t+3$ is approximately $p(cr|lb) = 5$ percent.[14] This is a rather small number, although relatively much bigger than the probability of a crisis in tranquil times, which is approximately 2 percent. The second and third columns use alternative definitions of a lending boom: cumulative growth of more than 30 or 40 percent. Here, both the conditional and unconditional probability of crisis increase while the probability of a

Table 3.3
Probability of a crisis

	LB2	LB3	LB4
Pr(crisis in $j+1$|LB $[j]$)	4.68	5.84	7.02
Pr(crisis in $j+2$|LB $[j]$)	5.26	6.57	7.89
Pr(crisis in $j+3$|LB $[j]$)	2.92	3.65	4.39
Pr(crisis in tranquil times)	1.71	3.30	3.55
Pr(LB|crisis $[j]$)	85.71	71.43	57.14

Notes: LB2–LB4 denote three different definitions of a lending boom. LB2 is a period of a cumulative increase in real credit over the past two years of more than 20 percent (30 percent for LB3 and 40 percent for LB4). Pr(crisis in $j+i$\|LB $[j]$) with $i = 1\dots3$ denotes the probability of a crisis during the year $j+i$. Pr(crisis in tranquil times) denotes the probability of a crisis in all other years. Pr(LB\|crisis $[j]$) denotes the probability that a lending boom was present within the three years before the crisis or during the year of the crisis.

lending boom, given a crisis, decreases. Overall, the argument does not change for different definitions of the lending boom.

Why Not Variance?
In the literature, variance is the typical measure of volatility. We choose not to use the variance of credit growth to identify growth-enhancing credit risk because a high variance reflects not only the presence of boom-bust cycles but also the presence of other, more frequently occurring shocks. Why is this the case? During boom-bust cycles, credit grows gradually during the boom phase and then abruptly falls during a crisis. Moreover, such a bust does not happen very often as crises are rare events. This pattern means that there is an outlier on the left side of the distribution of credit growth, which generates *negative skewness*. By contrast, if the shocks were not rare, *many* realizations of the sample would increase the mass under the left tail of the distribution and negative skewness would not exist.

Notice that both large and small shocks generate variance without generating skewness if they occur quite often. For this reason, variance may lead to false inferences about the links among liberalization, fragility, and growth. Variance is not a sufficient statistic for distinguishing economies that have followed risky, growth-enhancing credit paths from those that have experienced an abundance of other random shocks. In the sample we consider, this problem is particularly acute because smaller shocks in either direction are more abundant than the rare crises that punctuate lending booms.[15] By contrast, negative skewness of credit growth is an indicator that is able to discriminate between the two and that only picks up the incidence of occasional crises.[16]

So far we have focused on skewness, the third moment of the distribution, but what about higher moments—namely, kurtosis? Kurtosis could in principle provide further information about the distribution. First, note that skewness is sufficient to identify a risky path. High kurtosis may come on top of it, but it is neither necessary nor sufficient. The combination of skewness and kurtosis would also indeed be sufficient, but it identifies the extreme cases only. In practice, we find that it is not useful in identifying the risky and safe paths. For instance, it does not capture many countries that have experienced boom-bust cycles (such as Chile, Mexico, and Turkey). If there is a single, short-lived crisis, an outlier in the distribution leads to a long tail on the left and a high kurtosis. Yet if there is autocorrelation in the growth rates and the crisis is somewhat persistent, or if there is more than one crisis, the distribution becomes bimodal, and kurtosis can easily become quite low. It is therefore an excessively sensitive measure of bumpiness.[17]

In principle, one could argue that other rare shocks that do not originate in the credit market, affect both safe and risky economies. Hence, skewness could pick up countries that did not undertake growth-enhancing credit risk but had exogenous negative rare shocks that led to a negatively skewed distribution. We are not aware that such shocks have hit MICs during the last two decades.[18]

Financial Fragility and Growth

We have shown that trade liberalization is typically followed by financial liberalization, which in turn leads not only to financial deepening but also to booms and busts. On the one hand, in an economy with severe credit market imperfections, financial deepening is good for growth because financing constraints are eased. On the other hand, crises are bad for growth because they generate systemic insolvencies and fire sales. Ultimately, which of these two effects dominates is an empirical question. The following stylized fact, established by Ranciere, Tornell and Westermann (2003), summarizes the results that will be discussed below.

Stylized Fact 3.4 *Over the last two decades, when the standard variables are controlled for, countries with bumpy credit paths have grown faster than those with smooth credit paths.*

Our results are foreshadowed by figure 3.5, which shows the link between GDP growth and the moments of credit growth across MICs, controlling for initial GDP and population growth. Rapid long-run GDP growth is associated with a higher mean growth rate of credit, lower variance, and negative skewness.

As the figure shows, countries that have followed a risky path, such as Chile, Korea, and Thailand, exhibit negatively skewed credit growth and rapid GDP growth. In contrast, countries that have followed a safe path do not exhibit negative skewness and have slow growth; examples are Bangladesh, Morocco, and Pakistan. China and Ireland are notable exceptions: they have experienced extremely rapid GDP growth over the last twenty years, but have not experienced a major crisis despite a high rate of credit growth.

In order to assess the link between bumpiness and growth, we add the three moments of real credit growth to the regression in equation (3.1):

$$\Delta y_{it} = \lambda y_{i,\text{ini}} + \gamma X_{it} + \beta_1 \mu_{\Delta B, it} + \beta_2 \sigma_{\Delta B, it} + \beta_3 S_{\Delta B, it}$$

$$+ \phi_1 TL_{it} + \phi_2 FL_{it} + \varepsilon_{it}, \tag{3.2}$$

where Δy_{it}, $y_{i,\text{ini}}$, X_{it}, TL_{it}, and FL_{it} are defined as in equation (3.1), and $\mu_{\Delta B, it}$, $\sigma_{\Delta B, it}$, and $S_{\Delta B, it}$ are the mean, standard deviation, and skewness of the real credit growth rate, respectively. We do not include investment as a control variable because we expect the three moments of credit growth, our variables of interest, to affect GDP growth through higher investment.

We estimate equation (3.2) using the same type of overlapping panel data regression as for equation (3.1). For each moment of credit growth and each country, we construct ten-year averages starting with the period 1980–1989 and rolling forward to the period 1990–1999. Similarly, the liberalization variables take values in the interval [0, 1], depending on the proportion of liberalized years in a given window.[19] Given the dimension of equation (3.2), the overlapping-windows regression is the most appropriate method for the analysis we perform here.[20]

Table 3.4 reports the estimation results. Consistent with the literature, we find that after controlling for the standard variables, the mean growth rate of credit has a positive effect on long-run GDP growth, and the variance of credit growth has a negative effect. Both variables enter significantly at the 5 percent level in all regressions.[21]

The first key point established in panel A of table 3.4 is that the credit that accompanies rapid GDP growth is bumpy. Columns 1 and 2 show that bumpy credit markets are associated with higher growth rates across countries with functioning financial markets. That is, negative skewness—a bumpier growth path—is on average associated with faster GDP growth. This estimate is significant at the 5 percent level.[22]

To interpret the estimate of 0.27 for bumpiness, consider India, which has near 0 skewness, and Thailand, which has a skewness of

A. Growth and mean

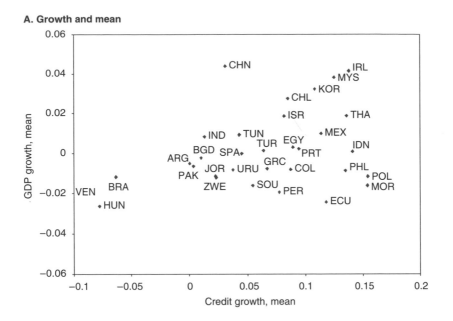

B. Growth and variance

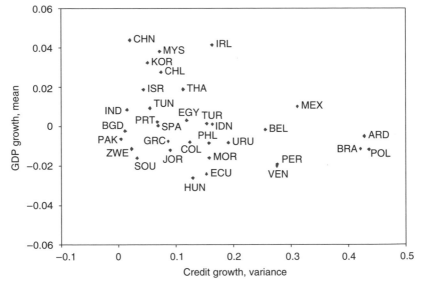

Figure 3.5
Moments of credit and GDP growth
Note: The graphs plot the moments of real credit growth during the period 1988–1999 against the residuals of a growth regression that controls for initial per capita GDP and population growth.

C. Growth and skewness

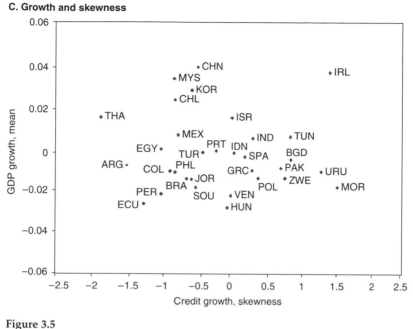

Figure 3.5
(continued)

−2. A point estimate of 0.27 implies that an increase in the bumpiness index of 2 (from 0 to −2) increases the average long-run GDP growth rate by 0.54 percentage point a year. Is this estimate economically meaningful? To address this question, note that after controlling for the standard variables, Thailand grows about 2 percentage points faster per year than India. Thus, about a quarter of this growth differential can be attributed to credit risk taking, as measured by the skewness of credit growth. One can interpret the negative coefficient on variance as capturing the effect of "bad" volatility generated by, for instance, procyclic fiscal policy.[23] Meanwhile, the positive coefficient on bumpiness captures the "good" volatility associated with the type of risk taking that eases financial constraints and increases investment. Notice that a country with high variance need not have negative skewness.[24]

Table 3.4
Regressions explaining growth in GDP per capita with moments of credit growth

Independent variable	1[a]	2[b]	3[a]	4[b]	
Panel A: Main regressions					
Mean of real credit growth rate	0.170** (0.012)	0.154** (0.009)	0.093** (0.007)	0.110** (0.009)	
Standard deviation of real credit growth rate	−0.029** (0.007)	−0.030** (0.003)	−0.014** (0.003)	−0.019** (0.004)	
Negative skewness of real credit growth rate	0.174** (0.069)	0.266** (0.021)	−0.095* (0.053)	0.135** (0.031)	
Financial liberalization			1.894** (0.122)	1.811** (0.163)	
Trade liberalization			0.838** (0.155)	0.895** (0.198)	
Summary statistics					
Adjusted R^{2c}	0.667	0.629	0.752	0.731	
Number of observations	269	424	253	408	
	5[d]	6[e]	7[f]	8[g]	9[h]
Panel B: Robustness					
Mean of real credit growth rate	0.051** (0.010)	0.130** (0.019)	0.065** (0.009)	0.123** (0.010)	0.127** (0.009)
Standard deviation of real credit growth rate	−0.027** (0.006)	−0.030** (0.007)	−0.001 (0.003)	−0.027** (0.004)	−0.032** (0.004)
Negative skewness of real credit growth rate	0.354** (0.071)	0.212** (0.097)	0.066** (0.025)	0.207** (0.036)	0.216** (0.037)
Summary statistics					
Adjusted R^{2c}	0.617	0.619	0.901	0.562	0.630
Number of observations	383	383	424	414	414

Notes: Equation (3.2) in the text is estimated using the panel data and the GLS; the dependent variable is the average annual growth rate of real GDP per capita. Standard errors are reported in parentheses and are adjusted for heteroskedasticity according to Newey and West (1987). Control variables include initial per capita income, secondary schooling, population growth, and life expectancy.

Table 3.4
(continued)

Source: Authors' regressions.
a. Sample includes MICs only.
b. Sample includes HICs and MICs.
c. The adjusted R^2 is likely to overestimate the share of the variance explained by our right-hand-side variables because of the overlapping nature of the regression. For adjusting the R^2, no method comparable to that of Newey and West for the standard errors exists, and therefore the values need to be interpreted carefully.
d. Same as column 2, but using the legal origin index of La Porta, Lopez de Silanes, and Zamarripa (2002) as instruments in a 2SLS regression.
e. Same as column 2, but using lagged values as instruments in a 2SLS regression.
f. Same as column 2, but including fixed effects.
g. Same as column 2, but excluding China.
h. Same as column 2, but excluding Ireland.
**Significant at the 5 percent level.

The second main point is that the association between bumpiness and growth does not imply that crises are good for growth. Crises are costly. They are the price that must be paid in order to attain faster growth in the presence of credit market imperfections. To see this, consider column 3 in table 3.4 When the financial liberalization indicator is included in the growth regression, bumpiness enters with a negative sign (and is significant at the 10 percent level). In the MIC set, given that there is financial liberalization, the lower the incidence of crises, the better. We can see the same pattern in the sample that includes HICs as well as MICs: the point estimate of bumpiness in column 4 is lower than that in column 2.[25]

In order to deal with the possible endogeneity of the skewness variable, panel B of table 3.4 reports estimation results of 2SLS regressions using as instruments the legal origin index of La Porta, Lopez de Silanes, and Zamarripa (2002) as well as lagged values of all variables in the regression. Furthermore, panel B reports results of regressions with fixed effects and those excluding China and Ireland, which may be driven by other factors. Our benchmark results are robust to these different estimation methods.

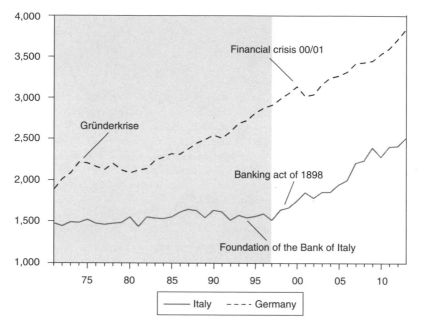

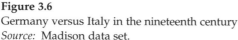

Figure 3.6
Germany versus Italy in the nineteenth century
Source: Madison data set.

As we stated at the beginning of this chapter, it is clear that liberalization without fragility is best, but the data suggest that this combination is not available to MICs. Instead, the existence of contract-enforceability problems implies that liberalization leads to higher growth because it eases financial constraints; but as a by-product, it also induces financial fragility. Despite the rare occurrence of crises, on net, financial liberalization has led to more rapid long-run growth, as shown by the estimates in tables 3.1 and 3.4.

Bumpiness and Growth in the Nineteenth Century

The link between bumpiness and growth also appears to be evident in the nineteenth century. Italy and Germany are clear examples.[26] While financial development started in Germany with the creation

A. Kernel densities

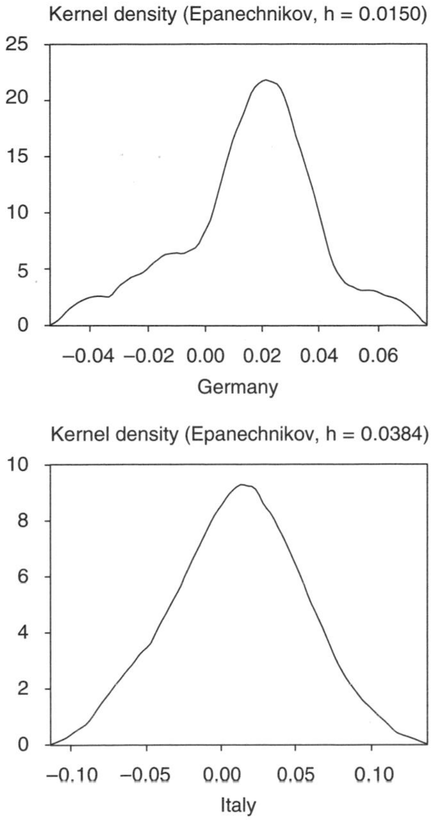

Kernel density (Epanechnikov, h = 0.0150)

Germany

Kernel density (Epanechnikov, h = 0.0384)

Italy

B. Descriptive statistics

	Germany	Italy
Mean	0.015983	0.011213
Standard deviation	0.022648	0.040670
Skewness	−0.440844	−0.096837

Figure 3.7
GDP growth distributions in Germany and Italy, 1871–1914
Note: The data are taken from the Madison data set.

of the banking system around 1850, Italy did not begin developing a banking system until the foundation of the Bank of Italy in 1893 and the Italian Banking Act in 1898.

Accordingly, Germany was on a high-growth path, but experienced two major crises: the so-called *Gründerkrise* (crisis of the founders) in 1873, and the 1900 financial crisis. Italy, on the other hand, exhibits only high-frequency noise without a major crisis until the beginning of financial development in the 1890s. Figure 3.6 plots the time path of real per capita GDP in the two countries. For a detailed description of the history of the two countries, see Borchardt (1982), Hoffmann (1965), and Zamagni (1993).

As we can see in figure 3.7, the distributions of output growth rates in Italy and Germany in the nineteenth century resemble those of India and Thailand today. Real output per capita in Germany grew by 1.6 percent on average, while in Italy it only grew by 1.1 percent. At the same time, output growth in Italy is characterized by a rather symmetrical distribution, while it is negatively skewed in Germany.

Looking at Italy before and after the beginning of financial development reveals the same pattern. Mean output growth increased from 0.006 percent on average during the stable period (1871–1898) to 3.5 percent during the risky period (1899–1913). Meanwhile, the skewness of output growth went from −0.06 to −0.40.

4   The Short Run: The Boom-Bust Cycles and the Credit Channel

In the previous chapter we saw that across MICs, there is a systematic link between growth and bumpiness over the long term—that is, the fastest-growing countries tend to experience booms and busts. In this chapter, we focus on the medium and short terms, zooming in for a close look at the commonalities among fast-growing MICs that might explain the bumpiness they experience along the way. As we shall see, in spite of the many ways in which MICs are distinct from one another, they have in common the strong responses of several macroeconomic variables to credit market shocks. We will show that at the heart of the amplifying mechanism is an asymmetrical sectoral response: the output of the bank-dependent N sector reacts more than T output. We also show that real exchange rate fluctuations play a key role in amplification.

First, we look at the boom-bust cycles that underlie the bumpiness associated with growth; as we shall see, the patterns followed by several macroeconomic variables around twin crises are remarkably similar across liberalized MICs despite differences in nominal exchange rate regimes. Importantly, along the typical cycle, credit comoves strongly with investment, the real exchange rate, and the ratio of N-to-T production.

We then demonstrate that the same comovements also arise more generally without conditioning on the occurrence of crises (that is, during tranquil times). Finally, we analyze in more detail the transmission mechanism by estimating VARs using quarterly data for several MICs. We find a strong credit channel, such that shocks to the spread between lending and foreign interest rates have a strong effect on GDP, and an even stronger effect on credit (see figure 4.9).[1]

We also find that in response to an increase in the spread, there is a decline in the N-to-T output ratio and a real depreciation (see figures 4.10 and 4.11). This second set of VARs identifies our amplification mechanism. In response to the increase in the spread, credit in the constrained N sector declines more than in the T sector and there is a real depreciation. The balance sheet effect implies that the real depreciation reduces the net worth of N agents with dollar debt on the books. This reduction allows them to borrow and invest even less, and so on.

Such an amplitude of the cycles and the strength of the comovements is not observed in HICs with well-developed financial markets, such as the United States. There is no evidence that MICs have systematically experienced frequent and severe exogenous shocks than HICs. This raises the question of what can explain the severity of the cycles and the comovements alluded to above—a question we will address in the next chapter, where we present the conceptual framework.

The Boom-Bust Cycle

The experiences of Mexico around the Tequila crisis and Thailand around the Asian crisis are prototypical examples of a boom-bust cycle. Here, we will show that several features of such boom-bust cycles are typical of MICs with liberalized financial markets. Some of the stylized facts that constitute a boom-bust cycle are widely agreed on, while others have only recently appeared in the literature or have been associated only with particular episodes.[2]

We characterize the boom-bust cycle by means of an event study on the set of MICs with functioning financial markets. By "functioning financial markets" we mean that the stock market must be an alternative source of finance for at least a subset of firms. The cycle is centered around twin crises during which a real exchange rate depreciation coincides with a banking crisis. The graphs below show the average behavior, across our set of thirty-five countries, of several macroeconomic variables around twin currency and banking crises during the period 1980–1999.[3] These graphs are the visual representations of the point estimates and standard errors from regressions in which the respective variable in each graph is the dependent variable, regressed on time dummies preceding and following a crisis. We say that there is a crisis at t if both currency and banking crises occur during year t, or if one occurs at t and the other at $t + 1$.[4]

The panel data estimations account for differences in the mean by allowing for fixed effects as well as differences in the variance using a GLS estimator. The heavy line represents the average deviation relative to tranquil times. The thin lines represent the 95 percent confidence interval.[5]

Many recent balance-of-payments crises have differed from their predecessors in that the currency crises have coincided with banking crises, and the main villains have not been such traditional suspects as fiscal or current-account deficits. Instead, credit and the real exchange rate have played the antagonists' roles.

Stylized Fact 4.1 *Twin crises are typically preceded by a real exchange rate appreciation and a lending boom along which bank credit grows unusually fast.*

Figure 4.1 shows that during the year prior to the crisis, the typical economy in an MIC experiences a 12 percent appreciation relative

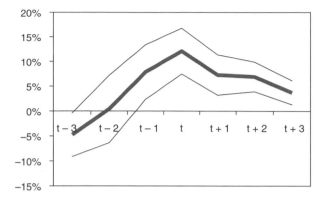

Figure 4.1
Real appreciation

to tranquil times, and that this appreciation is statistically significant.[6] Panel A of figure 4.2 illustrates the existence of a lending boom. During the three years prior to the crisis, the real credit growth rates are up to 3 percent higher than during tranquil times.

During the lending boom, banks fund themselves by borrowing abroad. Furthermore, they typically overexpose themselves to the N sector and do not hedge the implied real exchange rate risk. Even when banks denominate loans in foreign currencies, they face the risk that households and N-sector firms will not be able to repay in the event of a real depreciation. This is because in the event of a real depreciation, the debt burden will increase significantly in terms of domestic currency.

When twin crises hit, there is an average real depreciation of around 10 percent in the three years following the crisis. Since many agents, especially those in the N sector, will have denominated their debts in foreign currency during the boom years, the real depreciation has dramatic balance sheet effects: many agents see their debt values mushroom, while their revenues remain flat. As a result, their ability to service their debts is reduced and their

A. Real credit growth

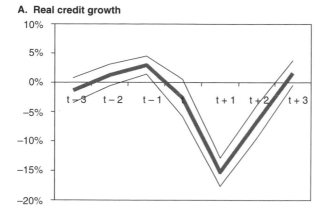

B. Real GDP growth

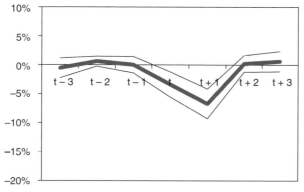

Figure 4.2
Real credit and GDP growth

net worth plummets. There is, therefore, a sharp deterioration of the banks' loan portfolios, and the banking system goes under.[7] To save the banking system, bailouts are granted, frequently with International Monetary Fund (IMF) support.[8] Despite this support, we find the following to be true:

Stylized Fact 4.2 *In the aftermath of a crisis there is a recession, which is typically short-lived.*

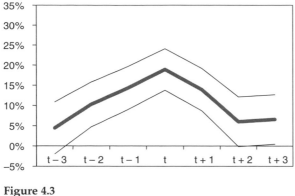

Figure 4.3
Credit/GDP

Moreover, a protracted credit crunch develops:

Stylized Fact 4.3 *In the aftermath of a crisis, credit falls more sharply than the GDP, and the gap widens over time even after economic growth has resumed.*

As we can see in panel B of figure 4.2, both during and the year after the crisis, the growth rate of the GDP is approximately 4 to 7 percent below its level during tranquil times, and by $t + 2$ the growth rate has already attained its tranquil-time mean growth rate. Adding the average tranquil-time GDP growth of 4 percent, it follows that the actual recession lasts for only one year $(t + 1)$.

Figure 4.3 shows that in the year after the onset of the crisis, credit falls more severely than the aggregate GDP. The puzzling fact is that the "credit crunch" becomes more severe through time: the credit-to-GDP ratio declines monotonically. Even by $t + 3$ there is no reversal of the credit crunch, although the downward trend stops. Put another way, from the onset of the crisis until $t + 3$, the GDP experiences a cumulative growth-rate loss of 10 percent, while the cumulative loss in real credit is about 20 percent. It is interesting, though, that not all of the financial-deepening gains made during the boom are lost during the bust, as suggested by the behavior of the credit-to-GDP ratio.

The puzzling coexistence of a protracted credit crunch and GDP growth several years after the crisis reflects the fact that the aggregate GDP performance masks an asymmetrical sectoral pattern:

Stylized Fact 4.4   *In the aftermath of a crisis, the T sector experiences an acceleration of growth after a mild recession, while the N sector experiences a sharp fall and sluggish recuperation. In contrast, prior to a crisis the N sector grows faster than the T sector.*

In the aftermath of a crisis, it seems as if the economy is doing well and deposit growth has resumed. Yet banks do not resume lending, perhaps because the meltdown that occurs during the crisis leads to poor capitalization of both the banks and the agents to whom they lend. The asymmetrical sectoral response indicates that the agents mainly affected are households as well as small and N-sector firms. Large and T-sector firms are not very dependent on bank credit, as they have access to other forms of external finance: trade credit, equity markets, and bond markets. In contrast, in MICs the N-sector agents are heavily dependent on bank credit, which is determined primarily by collateral values rather than investment opportunities.[9]

Figure 4.4 looks at the ratio of N-to-T production (N/T). As we can see, prior to the crisis, the N/T ratio is significantly above its tranquil-time level, while in the aftermath of the crisis, the N/T ratio follows a declining path. Interestingly, this path is quite similar to that followed by the credit-to-GDP ratio.

We proxy N-sector and T-sector production with data for construction, manufacturing, and services. The sector with a higher export share is considered T. Construction is never classified as T sector, while for services and manufacturing the choice between N and T varies across countries.[10]

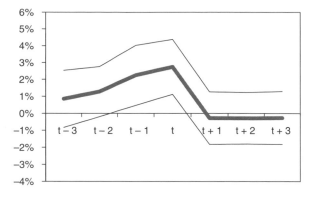

Figure 4.4
N-to-T output ratio

Stylized facts 3 and 4 suggest the following transmission mechanism. When the crisis hits, both the interest rate and the spread
jump. While large and T-sector firms are able to shift away from
bank credit to other forms of external finance, small and N-sector
firms are not. This results in a deterioration of the banks' credit
pool, which in turn feeds back into a higher spread. The outcome is
a protracted credit crunch, during which increases in the stock of
outstanding bank credit reflect mostly "evergreening," rather than
fresh, loans. Along this path, the T sector may initially suffer a mild
and short-lived decline, after which it will grow rapidly. The upshot
is that the N-to-T output ratio will decline even though the aggregate GDP increases.

In order to construct a theoretical explanation, it is important
to determine which components of the GDP drive the typical
boom-bust cycle. Is a twin crisis typically preceded by a consumption boom or an investment boom? Is there a big fiscal expansion
and/or a current account deterioration before a crisis? In answer to
these questions, we find evidence of the following stylized fact:

Stylized Fact 4.5 *Investment is the component of the GDP that
exhibits by far the largest (and statistically significant) deviations*

from tranquil times, while consumption deviations are quite mild and insignificant.

Panel A of figure 4.5 shows that investment exhibits a significantly higher growth rate of up to 14 percent during the three years prior to a crisis and a lower growth rate of up to 5 percent after the crisis, relative to its tranquil-time mean. For consumption, there is neither an increase before the crisis nor a decrease after the crisis (see panel B). Government expenditure is not significantly different, except for the years $t-2$, $t+2$, and $t+3$, when it is significantly higher by about 5 percent (panel D). Finally, exports are not significantly different from tranquil times either in the build-up period or the aftermath of a crisis (panel E).

To discriminate among models, it is also important to know whether crises are self-fulfilling or are generated by a large exogenous shock. It is difficult to determine whether a large exogenous shock was present. We looked to the usual suspects and found the following to be true:

Stylized Fact 4.6 *There is no significant deterioration in either the terms of trade or the U.S. interest rate in the year prior to the crisis.*

Does the Nominal Exchange Rate Regime Matter?

Stylized facts 1 through 6 complete our description of a boom-bust cycle. The question we address next is whether the properties of the boom-bust cycle vary across nominal exchange rate regimes, particularly whether it is true that only countries with fixed exchange rates experience these cycles. Although exchange rate regimes can be classified in several ways, including de facto versus de jure definitions, we have chosen not to focus on any given classification. Instead, we use a set of ten often-studied countries with a variety of nominal exchange rate regimes and exhibit the event windows for each.[11]

A. Investment

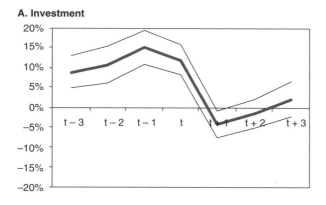

B. Consumption

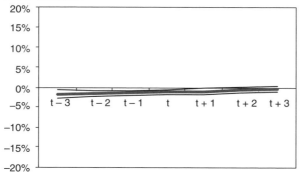

Figure 4.5
Components of GDP

Panels A and B of figure 4.6 show that from period $t - 3$ to period t, the terms of trade and the U.S. interest rate are not significantly different from their tranquil-time means. Of course, there might be other exogenous shocks that rock the boat, but the point is that neither the terms of trade nor the U.S. interest rate can be invoked to explain the occurrence of crises. Furthermore, to the best of our knowledge, no one has yet identified any exogenous shock as the cause of well-known crises, such as the Tequila or Asian crises.

To get an idea of the cross-country variation in nominal exchange rate regimes, we plot in panel A of figure 4.7 the nominal exchange

C. Export growth

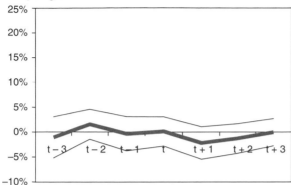

D. Government expenditure

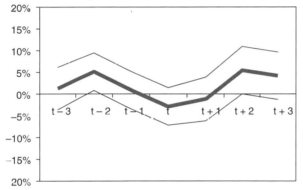

Figure 4.5
(continued)

rate around crisis dates.[12] We can see that in the run-up to crisis, there is a wide dispersion in the monthly variance of the nominal exchange rate. At one extreme we have Mexico, with a strict peg to the U.S. dollar and a monthly standard deviation of only 0.45 percent. At the other extreme we have Brazil, with a freely floating exchange rate and a monthly standard deviation of 8.39 percent. Thailand and Korea have quite stable exchange rates, while Peru and Sweden exhibit relatively more variability.[13]

A. Terms of trade

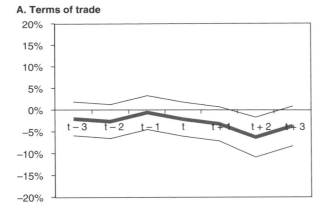

B. U.S. federal funds rate

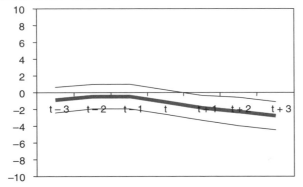

Figure 4.6
External shocks

Figure 4.7 depicts the three key variables we have focused on throughout this book: the credit-to-GDP ratio, the real exchange rate, and the N-to-T output ratio. The patterns of each country's credit-to-GDP ratios are strikingly similar to one another; also striking is the fact that in spite of the sharp cross-country differences in the paths of nominal rates, all countries experience a real exchange rate appreciation in the run-up to crisis and a sharp depreciation during the crisis. In the wake of crisis, all countries experience a fall

A. Nominal exchange rates

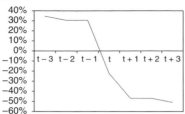

Mexico

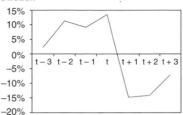

Sweden

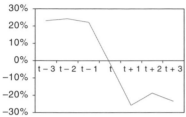

Thailand

The Philippines

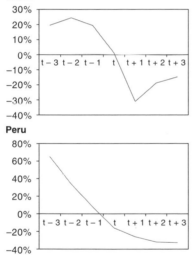

Korea

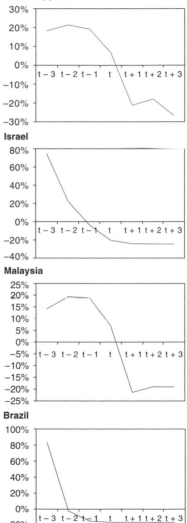

Israel

Peru

Malaysia

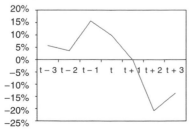

Finland

Brazil

Figure 4.7
Boom-bust cycles in countries with fixed and nonfixed exchange rates

B. Key variables of the boom-bust cycle

Credit/GDP   **1/real exchange rate**

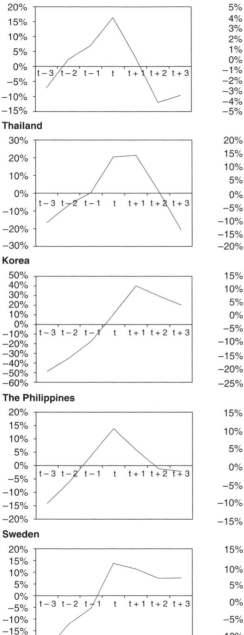
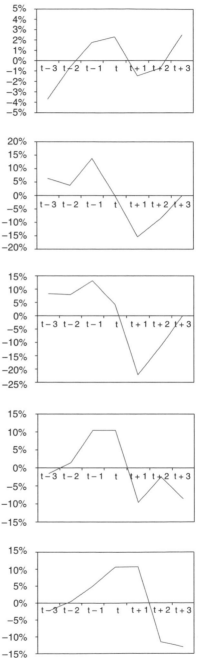

Figure 4.7
(continued)

N-to-T output ratio

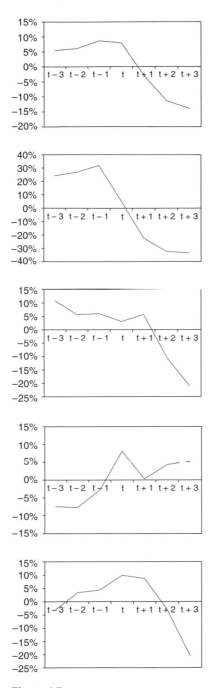

Figure 4.7
(continued)

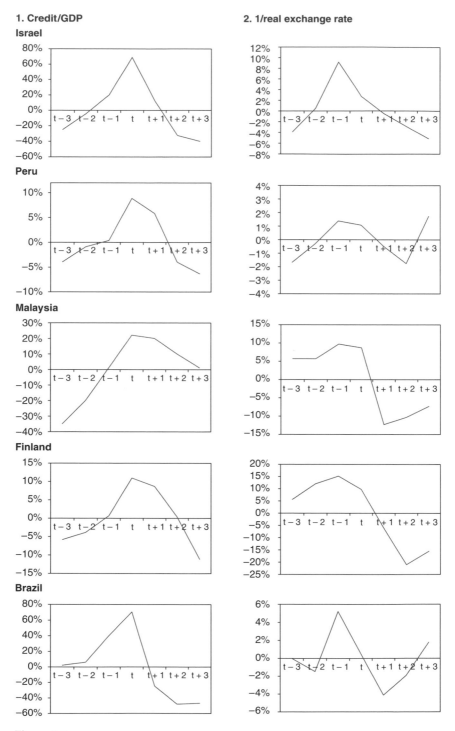

Figure 4.7
(continued)

3. N-to-T output

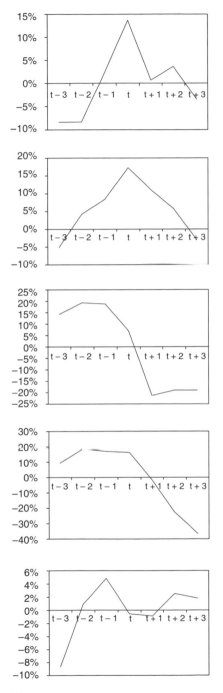

Figure 4.7
(continued)

in the N-to-T output ratio. This fall was sharp and protracted in all countries, except Brazil and the Philippines, where there is a mild rebound in the postcrisis period. This ratio never regains either its level before the crisis or the value it would have had if the boom had continued, however. Finally, we can see that in the run-up to crisis this ratio increases, except in Korea.

In sum, each of these three variables displays a pattern that is strikingly similar across all ten countries around crisis times. Thus, we reach the following conclusion:

Stylized Fact 4.7 *The boom-bust cycle under fixed exchange rates is not significantly different from the cycle under nonfixed regimes.*[14]

Comovements in Tranquil Times

The event windows of figures 4.1 to 4.7 show the behavior of several key variables around twin crises. Interestingly, the comovements of credit with several macrovariables observed along the boom-bust cycle are also evident in normal times. That is, even without conditioning on the occurrence of crises, credit growth comoves strongly with other macrovariables such as investment, the real exchange rate, and the N-to-T output ratio in MICs.

In this section, we give a first pass at the comovements by means of panel regressions over the period 1980–1999 on the same set of MICs for which we estimated the boom-bust cycle. The panel data estimation is implemented allowing for both fixed and random effects as well as a common intercept with neither of the two effects, and a GLS estimator.[15]

The first regression in panel A of table 4.1 shows that an increase in credit is associated with (1) a decline in the interest rate spread, (2) an increase in the ratio of N-to-T output, and (3) a real appreciation. It is remarkable that these partial correlations are highly significant across different specifications. Correlation (1) suggests the existence of a credit channel. Correlation (2) indicates that there exist balance sheet effects: in the presence of a currency mismatch, a real appreciation deflates the debt burden. This increases cash flow and the ability to borrow. Correlation (2) is consistent with the fact that the N sector is more "credit constrained" than the T sector.

A second set of regressions links credit growth to the components of the GDP. The results are displayed in panel B of table 4.1. What is surprising is the dog that didn't bark: consumption does not move with credit growth. Investment, in contrast, does vary strongly with credit. Furthermore, net exports have a significant negative correlation with credit, while government spending does not. All parameters, except those on consumption and government expenditure, are significant at the 5 percent level.

The partial correlations reported in table 4.1, of course, cannot be interpreted as *causal* relations. Yet it is noteworthy that a simple regression reveals the comovements to which we alluded earlier. Moreover, these comovements indicate which variables should be emphasized by theoretical models. These stylized facts indicate that a model of the economic fluctuations in MICs should generate an equilibrium path along which credit varies negatively with the spread and the real exchange rate, and positively with the N-to-T output ratio.

The Amplification Mechanism

In this section, we describe a mechanism that accounts for the boom-bust cycle and the correlations we have discussed; in the next chapter we present a formal argument.

For the present, consider a two-sector economy where T-sector agents have access to international financial markets, while the credit of N-sector agents is constrained by their net worth.[16]

Table 4.1
Comovements

Dependent variable: Real credit growth

	Common intercept	Fixed effects	Random effects
Panel A			
1/Real exchange rate	0.454**	0.342**	0.440**
	(0.085)	(0.074)	(0.082)
N/T output ratio	0.305**	0.249**	0.312**
	(0.134)	(0.074)	(0.128)
Interest rate spread	−0.002**	−0.002*	−0.002*
	(0.001)	(0.001)	(0.001)
Adjusted R^2	0.302	0.293	0.292
Number of countries	30	30	30
Panel B			
Investment	0.039**	0.036**	0.097**
	(0.017)	(0.018)	(0.034)
Consumption	−0.019	−0.032	−0.004
	(0.050)	(0.053)	(0.081)
Government expenditure	0.005	−0.005	−0.007
	(0.011)	(0.007)	(0.035)
Net exports	−0.082**	−0.074**	−0.090**
	(0.018)	(0.015)	(0.045)
Adjusted R^2	0.108	0.225	0.201
Number of countries	30	30	30

Notes: Standard errors are reported in parentheses; *indicates significance at the 10 percent level, **indicates significance at the 5 percent level, and ***indicates significance at the 1 percent level.

Furthermore, suppose for the moment that N-sector agents denominate their debt in foreign currency.[17]

Suppose there is a negative credit market shock that leads to higher debt service—for instance, a shock to expectations that is reflected in a higher domestic lending rate. Such a shock implies that firms without access to international financial markets can now borrow less at each level of net worth. Lower borrowing results in lower investment. This direct effect is amplified if there is currency mismatch, and part of the N sector's demand comes from the N sector itself. In this case, the fall in demand for N goods leads to a real depreciation. Since N-sector agents have dollar debt on the books, while their revenues are denominated in local currency, there is a fall in the N sector's profits and net worth. A vicious circle ensues as lower net worth leads to even lower investment, which leads to a lower demand for N goods and a steeper real depreciation, which leads to lower net worth, and so on. If the real depreciation is sharp enough, N-sector agents who have dollar debt on the books will go bust and a crisis will take place.

T-sector agents have access to international capital markets and can more easily substitute away from domestic borrowing. Thus, their decisions are mostly affected by the world interest rate, not the domestic lending rate. An increase in the spread between these two interest rates is therefore associated with a real depreciation, a decline in the N-to-T output ratio, and a fall in credit. The sectoral asymmetry also implies that the decline in GDP growth is milder than that of credit. This explains the persistent swings in the credit-to-GDP and the N-to-T output ratio observed along the typical boom-bust cycle. Furthermore, notice that even during tranquil times (that is, without conditioning on the occurrence of crises), the responses to shocks to the interest rate spread are consistent with the comovements we documented in table 4.1. An increase in the spread is associated with a fall in credit, the N-to-T output ratio, and GDP growth. If the output response in the N sector is not too large, there is also a real depreciation.

VAR Analysis: The Credit Channel

In Tornell and Westermann (2002b), we show how one can derive VARs from the risky equilibrium of an economy with an asymmetry in financing opportunities, like the economy described in

chapter 5. The equilibrium imposes unambiguous, contemporaneous linkages among key macroeconomic variables. This permits us
to identify our VARs: the equilibrium guides the choice of variables
and determines their ordering. This allows a structural interpretation of the impulse-response functions.

Using quarterly data for several MICs, we estimate these structural VARs and compute average impulse-response functions. The
first VAR includes the interest rate spread, the GDP, and credit.
The reaction of the GDP and credit to the spread will illustrate the
strength of the credit channel. In the second VAR, we include the
N-to-T output ratio instead of the GDP in order to see whether sectoral asymmetries play a significant role in the amplifying mechanism. The remaining two VARs are similar to the first two, except
that we include the real exchange rate instead of credit to determine
whether there is evidence of a balance sheet effect.

In choosing these specifications, we are mindful of the fact that
MICs have in common the existence of systemic guarantees and an
asymmetry in financing opportunities. There is a wide variation
across MICs, however, in exchange rate regimes and the prevalence
of nominal rigidities. It was thus important that the VARs be robust
to these institutional differences in order for them to apply across
the set of MICs. An attractive property of the risky equilibrium in
chapter 5 is that it is characterized by variables for which the equilibrium values are independent of these institutional differences.

We estimate the VARs in first differences using quarterly data for
eight MICs (Argentina, Brazil, Chile, Korea, Mexico, Peru, Thailand,
and Turkey) and the G3 countries (Germany, Japan, and the United
States), and compute the impulse-response functions corresponding
to a shock to the spread.[18] We include two lags and a time trend in
the estimation. Since we reject the null of cointegration among the
variables after finite sample adjustment, we do not include an
error-correction term (according to the finite sample critical values
reported in Cheung and Lai [1993]). In order to represent the

A. Medium-income countries

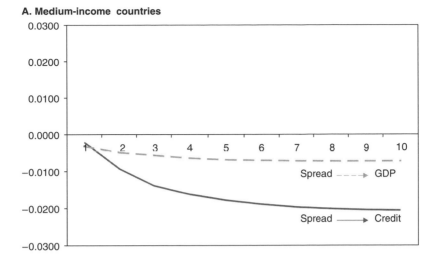

B. High-income countries

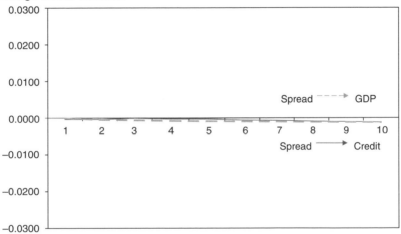

Figure 4.8a
VAR 1 $(\rho_t - r, b_t, GDP_t)$
Notes: The lines trace the accumulated average response of eight countries to a one-standard-deviation shock (which are computed from the forecast errors of the VAR). Calculations are based on three-variable VARs, including the spread, credit, and GDP. Each VAR is estimated from quarterly data in growth rates, allowing for two lags and a time trend.

Figure 4.8b
VAR 1 $(\rho_t - r, b_t, GDP_t)$
Notes: The lines trace the accumulated average response of three countries to a one-standard-deviation shock. Calculations are based on three-variable VARs, as specified in figure 4.8a.

C. Mexico versus United States

Mexico

Accumulated response of credit to a shock in the spread

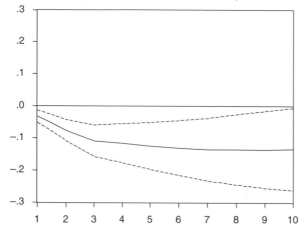

Accumulated response of GDP to a shock in the spread

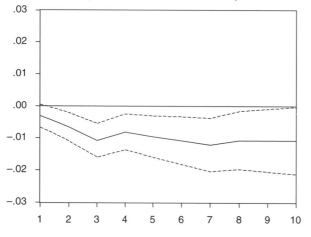

Figure 4.8c

VAR 1 $(\rho_t - r, b_t, GDP_t)$

Notes: The lines trace the accumulated response of Mexico and the United States to a one-standard-deviation shock. Calculations are based on three-variable VARs, as specified in figure 4.8a. Finite sample critical values are generated by one thousand Monte Carlo replications.

United States
Accumulated response of credit to a shock in the spread

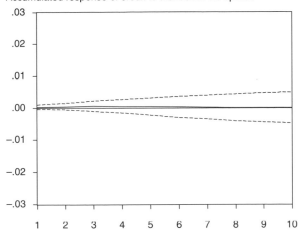

Accumulated response of GDP to a shock in the spread

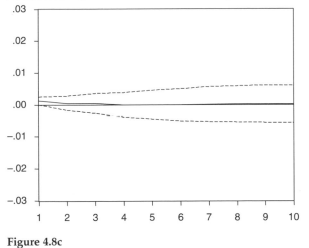

Figure 4.8c
(continued)

impulse-response functions in a visually illustrative way, we show
the grouped impulse-response functions that depict the average behavior of the eight countries—a representation also used in Bekaert,
Harvey, and Lundblad (2001).

The first VAR addresses the existence and the strength of the
credit channel. It includes the spread between the foreign and
domestic interest rates $(\rho_t - r)$, credit b_t, and the GDP. This ordering follows from the risky equilibrium described in Tornell and
Westermann (2002b), as $\rho_t - r$ is affected only by shocks to the
expected bailout rate, b_t is contemporaneously affected only by the
spread, and GDP_t is affected by the other two variables in the same
period.

Notice that the ordering of the variables is different than in the literature, where the interest rate and the spread are typically placed
in the last position of the VAR. The rationale for this ordering is
that if the central bank has full control over short-term rates, it can
immediately adjust them in response to an output shock. Thus, interest rates can be contemporaneously affected by output in quarterly data. While this might be the case in countries such as the
United States, it is not necessarily so in MICs, in which standard
monetary instruments such as open market operations often have
little leeway in affecting the interest rates that determine investment. Thus, output may not have a contemporaneous effect on the
spread.[19]

In MICs, shocks to the spread $\rho_t - r$ are more appropriately
viewed as shocks to agents' expectations about the willingness and
the ability of the government to guarantee loans. These, in turn, are
determined by, among other things, the fiscal stance of the government, its access to international credit lines, and the willingness of
politicians to grant bailouts.[20]

Figure 4.8 traces the cumulative response of the GDP and credit
to a one-standard-deviation shock in the spread. Shown are four
cumulative impulse response functions corresponding to an aver-

A. Middle-income countries

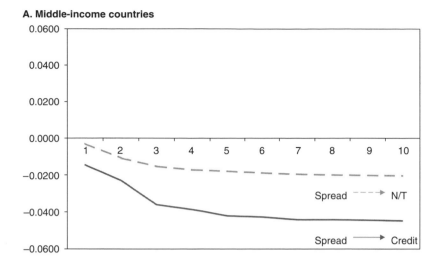

B. High-income countries

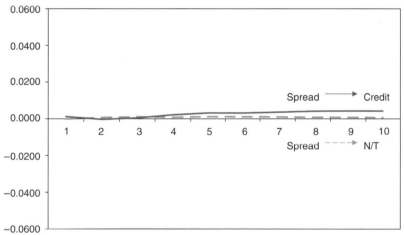

Figure 4.9a
VAR 2 $(\rho_t - r, b_t, p_t q_t^n / q_t^{tr})$
Notes: The lines trace the accumulated average response of eight countries to a one-standard-deviation shock. Calculations are based on three-variable VARs, including the spread, credit, and N/T. Each VAR is estimated from quarterly data in growth rates, allowing for two lags and a time trend.

Figure 4.9b
VAR 2 $(\rho_t - r, b_t, p_t q_t^n / q_t^{tr})$
Notes: The lines trace the accumulated average response of three countries to a one-standard-deviation shock. Calculations are based on three-variable VARs, as specified in figure 4.9a.

C. Mexico versus United States

Mexico

Accumulated response of credit to a shock in the spread

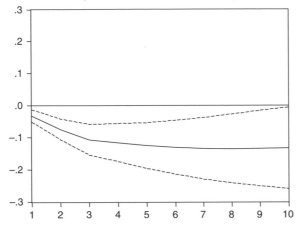

Accumulated response of N/T to a shock in the spread

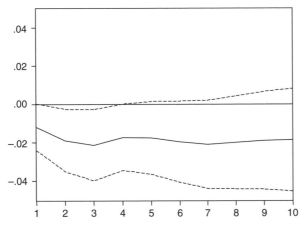

Figure 4.9c

VAR 2 $(\rho_t - r, b_t, p_t q_t^n / q_t^{tr})$

Notes: The lines trace the accumulated response of Mexico and the United States to a one-standard-deviation shock. Calculations are based on three-variable VARs, as specified in figure 4.9a. Finite sample critical values are generated by one thousand Monte Carlo replications.

United States
Accumulated response of credit to a shock in the spread

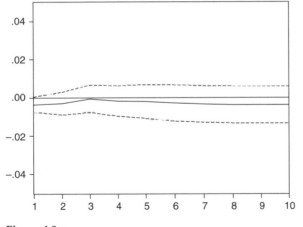

Accumulated response of N/T to a shock in the spread

Figure 4.9c
(continued)

age of the eight MICs (panel A), an average of the G3 (panel B), and a comparison of Mexico and the United States (panel C).

We can see that in the group of eight MICs, both variables respond negatively to the shock. By contrast, in the G3 the responses are an order of magnitude smaller, although they have the same sign. Panel C shows the point estimates and standard errors for the cases of Mexico and the United States. Here again, we see that the response in Mexico is much larger than in the United States. The responses in Mexico are also significant at the 5 percent level, while the ones in the United States are not.[21]

This result establishes that the credit channel is strong in MICs: the GDP reacts strongly to the interest rate spread. It also provides a hint as to the amplifying mechanism, as credit also reacts strongly to the spread—in fact, it reacts more strongly than the GDP. This observation is consistent with any model having a financial accelerator. At this point, however, we cannot discern any specific amplifying mechanism. The next group of VARs will help us uncover the mechanism that generates the strong credit channel.

The second group of VARs will permit us to discriminate between amplifying mechanisms wherein sectoral asymmetries play a significant role and other possible mechanisms. Panel A of figure 4.9 shows that in MICs, there is a striking asymmetry in the response of the N and T sectors. In response to a positive shock in the spread, credit and the N-to-T output ratio decline. Panel B shows that this amplifying mechanism is indeed a phenomenon particular to MICs, as we do not see a similar pattern in the G3. Panel C shows the impulse-response functions for Mexico and the United States. Here again, the reaction of credit and the N-to-T ratio are statistically significant in Mexico, but not in the United States.

The fall in the N-to-T output ratio in response to the shock establishes our second main finding: that an asymmetry in sectoral responses is a key element of the amplifying mechanism in MICs. Any model that aims to explain the amplification of credit market

A. Middle-income countries

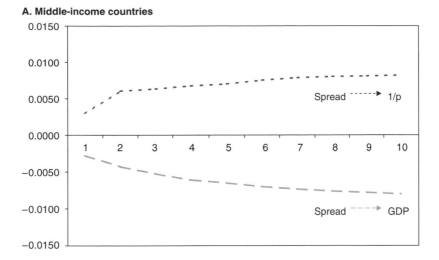

B. High-income countries

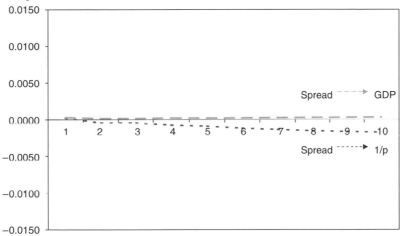

Figure 4.10a
VAR 3 $(p_t - r, 1/p_t, GDP_t)$
Notes: The lines trace the accumulated average response of eight countries to a one-standard-deviation shock. Calculations are based on three-variable VARs, including the spread, $1/p$, and GDP. Each VAR is estimated from quarterly data in growth rates, allowing for two lags and a time trend.

Figure 4.10b
VAR 3 $(p_t - r, 1/p_t, GDP_t)$
Notes: The lines trace the accumulated average response of three countries to a one-standard-deviation shock. Calculations are based on three-variable VARs, as specified in figure 4.10a.

C. Mexico versus United States

Mexico

Accumulated response of 1/p to a shock in the spread

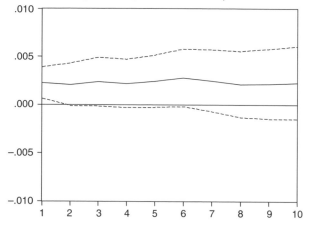

Accumulated response of GDP to a shock in the spread

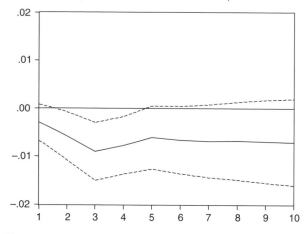

Figure 4.10c

VAR 3 $(\rho_t - r, 1/p_t, GDP_t)$

Notes: The lines trace the accumulated response of Mexico and the United States to a one-standard-deviation shock. Calculations are based on three-variable VARs, as specified in figure 4.10a. Finite sample critical values are generated by one thousand Monte Carlo replications.

United States
Accumulated response of 1/p to a shock in the spread

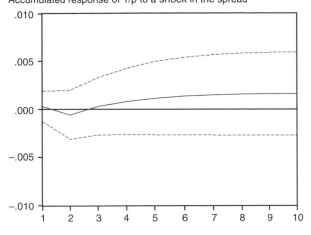

Accumulated response of GDP to a shock in the spread

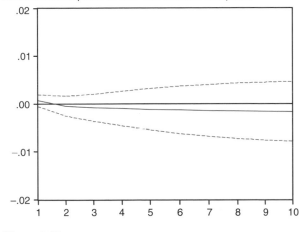

Figure 4.10c
(continued)

shocks in MICs also needs to explain the asymmetry in sectoral responses. In the mechanism we propose, this asymmetry is caused by an asymmetry in financing opportunities, as the N sector is more credit constrained than the T sector.

If the fact that both credit and the N-to-T output ratio fall in response to the shock is associated with the sectoral asymmetry in financing opportunities, then this also explains why the credit response is stronger than that of the GDP in the first VAR. The response of the GDP reflects not only the decline in the N sector but also the mild response of the T sector to the spread.

The third group of VARs includes the real exchange rate $(1/p_t)$. These VARs allow us to analyze more directly the role played by the balance sheet effect in amplifying the direct effect of the spread on output.[22]

Figure 4.10 exhibits the cumulative impulse responses associated with the VAR $(p_t - r, 1/p_t, GDP_t)$. For the group of MICs, there is a decline in the GDP and a real depreciation in response to a positive shock to the spread. In the G3, however, this response is absent. The graphs for Mexico and the United States replicate the same patterns.

Figure 4.11 corresponds to a VAR that includes the N-to-T output ratio instead of the GDP. Here again, we see a clear asymmetrical response of the two sectors in the group of MICs and in Mexico. Such an asymmetry is nevertheless absent in the grouped responses of the G3 and in the United States.

We take the significant real depreciation in response to an increase in the spread as an indication that currency mismatch may be a key ingredient of the amplifying mechanism. The balance sheet effect is at work: after the initial decline in N investment, the real depreciation reduces the net worth of N agents with dollar debt on the books. This reduction allows them to invest even less, and so on.

A. Middle-income countries

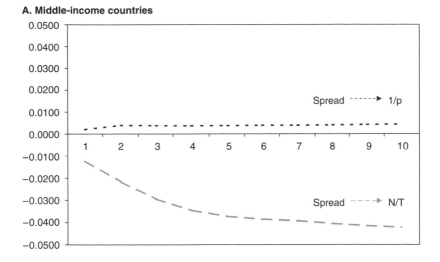

Spread - - - → 1/p

Spread - - - → N/T

B. High-income countries

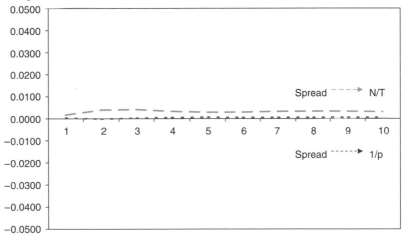

Spread - - - → N/T

Spread - - - → 1/p

Figure 4.11a

VAR 4 $(\rho_t - r, 1/p_t, p_t q_t^n / q_t^{tr})$

Notes: The lines trace the accumulated average response of eight countries to a one-standard-deviation shock. Calculations are based on three-variable VARs, including the spread, $1/p$, and N/T. Each VAR is estimated from quarterly data in growth rates, allowing for two lags and a time trend.

Figure 4.11b

VAR 4 $(\rho_t - r, 1/p_t, p_t q_t^n / q_t^{tr})$

Notes: The lines trace the accumulated average response of three countries to a one-standard-deviation shock. Calculations are based on three-variable VARs, as specified in figure 4.11a.

C. Mexico versus United States

Mexico

Accumulated response of 1/p to a shock in the spread

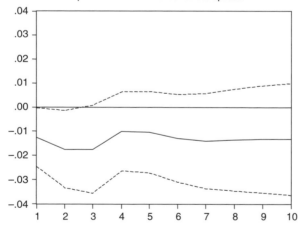

Accumulated response of N/T to a shock in the spread

Figure 4.11c

VAR 4 $(\rho_t - r, 1/p_t, p_t q_t^n / q_t^{tr})$

Notes: The lines trace the accumulated average response of Mexico and the United States to a one-standard deviation shock. Calculations are based on three-variable VARs, as specified in figure 4.11a. Finite sample critical values are generated by one thousand Monte Carlo replications.

United States
Accumulated response of 1/p to a shock in the spread

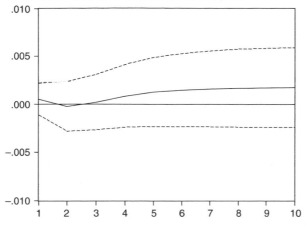

Accumulated response of N/T to a shock in the spread

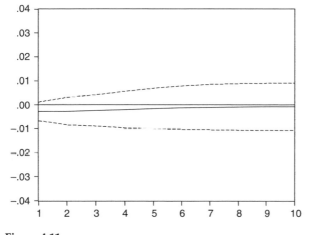

Figure 4.11c
(continued)

Related Literature

There is a vast literature concerning the effects of credit market
shocks on output. This section is related to the subset of this literature that is devoted to the credit channel. Investigations into
whether monetary policy affects output through a credit channel, in
addition to the traditional money channel, have focused on the link
between interest rate spreads and future movements in output. This
link has been established in U.S. data by Stock and Watson (1989)
as well as Friedman and Kuttner (1993). Bernanke, Gertler, and
Gilchrist (2000) show that this link is consistent with the existence
of a financial accelerator and that the spread is an indicator of the
stance of monetary policy. Bernanke (1990), however, finds that the
strength of this link has been declining over time, and Friedman
and Kuttner (1998) point out that the spread failed to predict the
1990 recession. In related work, Kashyap, Stein, and Wilcox (1993)
consider the mix of loans and commercial paper to investigate the
existence of the credit channel.

The VARs we derive and estimate are similar to those in the literature in that they link a spread with a measure of output. There
are several differences, though. We include variables that measure
asymmetrical sectoral patterns: the N-to-T output ratio and the real
exchange rate. Also, we include the difference between the domestic
lending rate and the world interest rate, which is the relevant
spread in the presence of currency mismatch and a sectoral asymmetry in financing opportunities.[23]

With regard to identification, the ordering of our VARs follows
directly from the equilibrium of an economy like that described in
chapter 5. As the model implies, the spread is not allowed to respond to GDP surprises within a quarter. In MICs, the monetary
authority has little leeway to influence the spread through standard
open market operations. Instead, changes in the spread mainly re-

flect changes in the anticipated generosity of the guarantees. The expected generosity, in turn, depends on the ability and the willingness of the government to cover the guarantees. Clearly, these factors cannot be changed at short notice in response to a quarterly GDP surprise.

In order to uncover the propagation mechanism in the United States, a series of papers look at the asymmetrical behavior of small and large firms. Gertler and Gilchrist (1994) find that in the manufacturing sector, small firms react more strongly to monetary contractions than large firms do. This evidence is associated with the fact that large firms are less bank dependent and make greater use of equity and bond markets. Ramey (1993) finds that the ratio of credit to small and large firms has some effect on aggregate output. Kashyap and Stein (2000) discover that after a contractionary monetary shock, lending of small banks declines more strongly than that of large banks. They argue that—as with small firms—small banks have more difficulty in accessing uninsured sources of funds. The asymmetry between small and large agents is also key in MICs. Nevertheless, in MICs this asymmetry also distinguishes the N and T sectors. Using World Bank survey data at the firm level, we will document in the following chapter that most small firms are in the N sector, while most large firms are in the T sector.[24]

Conclusion

The evidence presented in this chapter shows that in spite of the many ways in which MICs are distinct from one another, they have in common the strong responses of several macroeconomic variables to credit market shocks. In particular, we have seen that the behavior of credit is crucial to understanding the boom-bust cycle. In addition, the VARs support the view that an increase in the spread between domestic and international interest rates has a strong effect on the GDP, and an even stronger effect on domestic credit; the spread also has a strong effect on the real exchange rate and the ratio of N-to-T output.

We have argued that the strength of the response to shocks is linked to an asymmetry in financing opportunities across the N and T sectors, and to a severe currency mismatch. As a result, movements in the real exchange rate play an amplifying role through their effects on balance sheets. Of course, we are not ruling out alternative mechanisms, but we are unaware of any that is capable of explaining simultaneously all of the regularities we have documented.

An implication of our findings is that sectoral indicators may be as crucial as aggregate ones for understanding MIC performance. Increases in the aggregate GDP driven by T firms may hide a languishing domestic sector, raising the prospect of future bottlenecks choking off growth. It follows that in a world of financial liberalization and asymmetries in financing opportunities across N and T sectors, stabilization policies should concentrate not only on inflation and the output gap but also on indicators such as credit growth and asymmetries in sectoral responses.[25] In chapter 5, we present a model that formalizes these ideas.

5   The Conceptual Framework

In this chapter, we present a model that helps explain why many middle-income countries (MICs) exhibit fluctuations of a much greater magnitude than those observed in high-income countries (HICs), even though MICs have not been hit by either more severe or more frequent shocks than have HICs. In particular, the model will account for the boom-bust cycles and the strong credit channel typically observed in MICs. We will then use this model of economic fluctuations in MICs to address the question of whether financial liberalization is good for growth and welfare despite the occurrence of crises. The material in this chapter is based on the models of Schneider and Tornell (2004), and Ranciere, Tornell, and Westermann (2003).

The evidence presented in this book indicates that credit market imperfections are at the heart of the large fluctuations in MICs. In the model we will present below, imperfections prevalent in MICs interact to generate strong amplification and boom-bust cycles. We will then embed the model in an endogenous growth setup and explain why financial liberalization leads to higher growth yet also, as a by-product, makes the economy prone to crises.

Before jumping to the argument of how certain credit market imperfections can generate a boom-bust cycle like the one we have documented in chapter 4, let us discuss which ingredients are necessary. First, notice that in order for banking crises to coincide with real depreciations, to be preceded by lending booms and followed by credit crunches, it is necessary that borrowing constraints arise in equilibrium and, at the same time, that agents take on credit risk so that financial fragility arises. If either the constraints or the fragility were not present, the model would be unable to generate such boom-bust episodes.

Second, another key property of the MIC cycles is the asymmetrical sectoral response: the N-to-T output ratio increases during the boom, falls sharply during the crisis, and continues declining during the credit crunch. Crucial to generating this asymmetrical pattern is modeling an asymmetry in financing opportunities between the T and N sectors. In chapter 6, we document the existence of such an asymmetry: most T-sector firms can finance themselves in international markets, while most N-sector firms are financially constrained and bank dependent.

To explain some aspects of the typical boom-bust cycle, third-generation crisis models have looked to financial market imperfections as fundamentals. The models are typically based on one of two distortions: either "bad policy," in the form of bailout guarantees, or "bad markets," in the form of a credit market imperfection that induces balance sheet effects (such as asymmetrical information or the imperfect enforceability of contracts). The former distortion leads to excessive risk taking, while the latter gives rise to borrowing constraints. In the literature, either borrowing constraints or credit risk arise in equilibrium, but not both at the same time; yet as we explained above, to account for a boom-bust cycle it is necessary to have both. In general, however, the forces that generate endogenous credit risk also neutralize the forces that give rise to borrowing constraints.

In this chapter, we tackle this problem by using a simplified version of the model of Schneider and Tornell (2004). Then we look at the long run, and use the model of Ranciere, Tornell, and Westermann (2003) to establish a positive link between growth and the incidence of boom-bust cycles.

A Heuristic Argument

Before we proceed to the next section, where we present the model itself, it may be helpful to describe the model heuristically. Consider a two-sector economy that is subject simultaneously to the bad policy and bad market distortions to which we've alluded. We will show that their interaction gives rise to both borrowing constraints (in which lending is constrained by firms' cash flow) and credit risk (in which agents choose the "wrong" debt denomination: dollars instead of pesos [currency mismatch]). Furthermore, the equilibrium path of such an economy delivers a dynamic account of a complete boom-bust episode without the need to assume exogenous shocks.

The model captures the asymmetry in financing opportunities by considering an economy where T-sector firms have access to perfect financial markets, while N-sector firms are run by managers who face two credit market imperfections. First, they cannot commit to repay debt (that is, managers can divert funds to themselves by incurring a cost). Second, lenders enjoy *systemic bailout guarantees*. It is a stylized fact that governments ensure creditors against systemic crises. That is, if a critical mass of borrowers is on the brink of bankruptcy, the government will implement policies to ensure that creditors get repaid (at least in part) and thus avoid an economic meltdown. These policies may come in the form of an easing of monetary policy, the maintenance of an exchange rate peg, or the handing out of checks.[1]

We will assume that the goods produced by the N sector are used as inputs in both the T and the N sector. Meanwhile, the T sector produces final consumption goods. As we shall see, the assumption that N goods are demanded by the N sector is key for the amplification mechanism and the occurrence of self-fulfilling crises; that N goods are used as inputs in T production is crucial for the point that higher N-sector growth helps the T sector grow faster. In contrast, the assumption that the T sector produces final consumption goods is not necessary.

In order to describe the amplification mechanism, suppose for the moment that N-sector agents face borrowing constraints and denominate their debt in foreign currency (that is, T goods). In such an economy, an increase to the domestic lending rate (that can be caused by a shock to expectations) leads to higher debt service and thus implies that firms without access to international financial markets can now borrow less at each level of net worth. Lower borrowing results in lower investment. This direct effect is amplified because there is currency mismatch and part of the N sector's demand comes from the N sector itself. Therefore, the fall in demand for N goods leads to a real depreciation. Since N-sector agents have dollar debt on the books, while their revenues are denominated in local currency, there is a fall in the N sector's profits and net worth. A vicious circle ensues as lower net worth leads to even lower investment, which leads to a lower demand for N goods and a steeper real depreciation, which leads to lower net worth and so on. In some circumstances, the real depreciation can be large enough so as to bankrupt all N-sector firms with T debt on the books. As a result, twin currency and banking crises will take place.

T-sector agents have access to international capital markets and can more easily substitute away from domestic borrowing. Thus, their decisions are mostly affected by the world interest rate, not by the domestic lending rate. An increase in the *spread* between these two interest rates is therefore associated with a fall in credit, a decline in the N-to-T output ratio, and a real depreciation—that is, a fall in the relative price of N goods. Furthermore, the sectorial asymmetry implies that the decline in GDP growth is milder than that of credit. This explains the persistent swings in the credit-to-GDP and the N-to-T output ratios observed in the data.

One question remains: How can borrowing constraints and currency mismatch arise simultaneously in equilibrium? The answer relies on the interaction of contract enforceability problems and systemic bailout guarantees. Enforceability problems generate borrowing constraints because this is the way in which lenders ensure they will be repaid. In order for guarantees not to neutralize the effects of enforceability problems, it is necessary that they be systemic, not unconditional. The latter are granted whenever there is a default by an individual borrower, while the former are granted only if a critical mass of borrowers goes bust. Clearly, if all debt were covered by unconditional bailout guarantees, then the enforceability problem would become irrelevant and borrowing constraints would not arise in equilibrium. Since a lender would be bailed out in the case of an idiosyncratic default, that lender does not have incentives to limit the amount of credit one extends to an individual borrower. In contrast, if the guarantees are systemic, they do not ensure lenders against idiosyncratic default by an individual firm. To credibly abstain from stealing, an individual manager must therefore respect a borrowing constraint, so that lenders are repaid in the good state where a bailout does not take place.

If the expected generosity of the guarantee is large enough, borrowers will find it optimal to take on *insolvency risk*. By doing so, they can cash in on the subsidy implicit in the guarantee, as the government will pay the debt obligation in case of insolvency. If the real exchange rate is expected to be sufficiently variable, currency mismatch is a prime vehicle for N-sector agents to take on insolvency risk. By denominating their debt in foreign currency, N-sector agents will pay extremely low interest rates as someone else will repay creditors in case of a sharp real depreciation.

Along the equilibrium path, there is a self-reinforcing mechanism that generates systemic insolvency risk. On the one hand, if N-sector firms expect the real exchange rate to fluctuate enough, they find it optimal to create a currency mismatch and thereby risk going bankrupt in case of depreciation. If all firms go bankrupt in case of a sharp depreciation, a bailout is triggered and debt repayment is shifted to the taxpayer. This increases ex ante profits. On the other hand, if there is a currency mismatch, a balance sheet effect validates firms' initial expectations of real exchange rate fluctuations.

The dynamic path of this economy delivers a complete boom-bust cycle. As in the data, model crises are preceded by a real appreciation as well as a lending boom. The boom features high leverage and risk taking by way of debt denomination by firms in the N sector. As a result, the economy becomes vulnerable to a self-fulfilling depreciation. In the aftermath of a crisis, the wealth of the N sector collapses. This generates a credit crunch that affects mainly the N sector and leads to a fall in the N-to-T output ratio, as observed in the data.

Armed with this boom-bust-cycle model, we now turn to the question of why financial liberalization leads both to higher long-run growth and a greater incidence of crises. In order to address this question, we need a stochastic growth model wherein crises can occur from time to time. To obtain such a model, and at the same time capture the high-frequency fluctuations observed in the data, Ranciere, Tornell, and Westermann (2003) embed the boom-bust-cycle model we have just described into an endogenous growth model. The model establishes a causal link from liberalization to growth, and shows how, in the presence of credit market imperfections, the forces that lead to higher growth also generate financial fragility.

Consider the two-sector economy we described above, where N goods are used as inputs in both the N and T sectors, and where there is an asymmetry in financing opportunities. In such an economy, trade liberalization increases GDP growth by promoting T-sector productivity. Financial liberalization adds even more to GDP growth by accelerating financial deepening, thereby increasing the investment of financially constrained firms. As we have seen, however, the easing of financial constraints is associated with the undertaking of credit risk, which often takes the form of foreign currency–denominated debt backed by N output. Credit risk arises because financial liberalization not only lifts restrictions that preclude risk taking but is also associated with explicit and implicit systemic bailout guarantees that cover creditors against systemic crises. Not surprisingly, an important share of capital inflows takes the form of risky bank flows, and the economy as a whole becomes financially fragile and experiences occasional crises.

Since N goods serve as intermediate inputs for both sectors, the N sector constrains the long-run growth of the T sector and that of GDP: there is a bottleneck. The undertaking of credit risk eases borrowing constraints and allows N-sector firms to invest more. High N-sector growth, in turn, helps the T sector grow faster by providing abundant and cheap inputs. Thus, as long as a crisis does not occur, growth in a risky economy is greater than in a safe one. Of course, financial fragility implies that a self-fulfilling crisis may occur. And during crises, GDP growth falls. Crises must be rare, however, in order to occur in equilibrium—otherwise agents would not find it profitable to take on credit risk in the first place. Average long-run growth is therefore greater along a risky path than a safe one even if there are large crisis costs.

Having a microfounded model permits an explicit welfare analysis and establishes conditions under which the welfare costs of crises are outweighed by the benefits of higher growth generated by financial liberalization. Because both sectors compete every period for the available supply of N goods, when contract enforceability problems are severe the N sector attains low leverage and commands only a small share of N inputs. This results in a socially inefficient, low-growth path: a central planner would increase the N-sector investment share to attain the Pareto optimal allocation. Clearly, the first best can be attained in a decentralized economy by reducing the agency problems that generate the financing constraints. If such a reform is not feasible, however, credit risk may be a second-best instrument to increase social welfare despite financial fragility. Ranciere, Tornell, and Westermann (2003) show that when contract enforceability problems are severe—but not too severe—and crisis costs are not excessively large, credit risk increases social welfare and brings the allocation nearer to the Pareto optimal level. Furthermore, T-sector agents will find it profitable to fund the fiscal cost of the guarantees. The funding of the guarantees actually effects a redistribution from the nonconstrained T sector to the constrained N sector. This redistribution is to the mutual benefit of both sectors.

These results imply that in the presence of severe credit market imperfections, financial liberalization is welfare improving only if it leads to financial fragility, which makes the economy prone to booms and busts. Clearly, these results do not imply that liberalization can attain the first best. The latter is attained by eliminating the enforceability problems that generate borrowing constraints. This requires the implementation of judicial reform, which is easier said than done.

This is as far as simple intuition can bring us. Since the real exchange rate is determined in general equilibrium, we need the aid of the model to guide our intuition as to when financing constraints and systemic endogenous risk can coexist. Some restrictions will have to be imposed on the parameters to ensure that the right balance exists between the opposing forces at work in this economy. The question then becomes one of whether these parameter restrictions generate an equilibrium path that exhibits the patterns typical of MICs.

The Model

Here, we formalize the intuitive argument described in the previous section and demonstrate that it is indeed part of an internally consistent story. We first show that the interaction of enforceability problems and bailout guarantees can generate a boom-bust cycle.

We then look at the long run, establishing a link between financial liberalization, growth, and the incidence of boom-bust cycles. At the end of the chapter, we sketch the argument that links liberalization and welfare. The first part of the model is based on Schneider and Tornell (2004), while the second part is based on Ranciere, Tornell, and Westermann (2003).[2]

The equilibrium will allow us to give a structural interpretation to the regressions of chapter 3, as it will establish a causal link from financial liberalization to financial fragility to growth, and it will impose restrictions on the sample of countries over which the mechanism operates. Furthermore, the equilibrium path of credit, the real exchange rate, and the N-to-T output ratio will account for the typical boom-bust cycle experienced by MICs, and will permit a structural interpretation to the VARs we estimate in chapter 4.

We consider a simple, dynamic general equilibrium model of an economy with two sectors: a T sector that produces the consumption good, and an N sector that produces an intermediate good that is used as an input in the production of both T- and N-sector goods. As we shall see, the fact that the N sector demands its own goods is necessary for financial fragility to arise in equilibrium; and the assumption that T production uses N inputs is key to generate the bottleneck effect and link financial fragility to higher GDP growth.[3]

We will denote the relative price of N goods (that is, the inverse of the real exchange rate) by $p_t = p_t^N/p_t^T$.[4] T goods are produced using an N input (d_t) according to $y_t = a_t d_t^{\alpha}$, where a_t is a technological parameter and $\alpha \in (0,1)$. In any equilibrium, it follows that T output and the T-sector demand for N goods are, respectively,

$$y_t = a_t d_t^{\alpha}, \quad d(p_t) = \left(\frac{\alpha a_t}{p_t}\right)^{1/(1-\alpha)}. \tag{5.1}$$

Notice that α is the share of N inputs in T production. N goods are produced using N goods as inputs (I_t) according to

$$q_{t+1} = \theta I_t. \tag{5.2}$$

The investable funds of an N firm consist of the debt that it issues (B_t) plus its cash flow (w_t). The firm's budget constraint, in terms of T goods, is thus

$$p_t I_t = w_t + B_t. \tag{5.3}$$

In order to allow for the possibility of financial fragility, we assume that there are two one-period debt instruments: N debt (b_t^n), which promises to repay in N goods, $p_{t+1}(1 + \rho_t^n)b_t^n$; and T debt (b_t), which promises to repay in T goods, $(1 + \rho_t)b_t$. Thus, the total debt in terms of T goods is $B_t = b_t + b_t^n$.

We can interpret T(N) debt as foreign (domestic) currency–denominated debt. As we shall see, the real exchange rate may take two values in equilibrium: a high and a low one. Since N-sector firms produce N goods and real exchange rate fluctuations are the only source of uncertainty, N debt is a perfect hedge, while T debt may be risky as it might lead to bankruptcy.[5]

In modeling the N sector, we will make two assumptions to capture the key features of MICs we discussed earlier. First, N-sector financing is subject to contract enforceability problems. Second, there are systemic bailout guarantees that cover lenders against systemic meltdowns.[6] We follow Schneider and Tornell (2004) and model the contract enforceability problem by assuming that firms are run by dynasties of two-period lived managers who cannot commit to repay debt.

Contract Enforceability Problem   If at time t the young manager incurs a nonpecuniary cost $h[w_t + B_t]$, then at $t + 1$ that manager will be able to divert all the returns, provided the firm is solvent.

Lenders finance only those plans that do not lead to diversion. Thus, when deciding whether to lend, they take into account that the goal of every manager is to maximize next period's expected profits net of diversion costs.

The firm is solvent next period if revenues $q_{t+1}p_{t+1}$ are no lower than the promised debt repayment $L_{t+1} = (1 + \rho_t)b_t + p_{t+1}(1 + \rho_t^n)b_t^n$ plus the young manager's wage $(1 - \beta)p_{t+1}q_{t+1}$. In this case, the old manager distributes the remaining profits, $\pi_{t+1} = \beta q_{t+1}p_{t+1} - L_{t+1}$, as a dividend to oneself. To capture the costs of financial melt-downs, we assume that under insolvency, a large share $1 - \mu_w$ of revenues are dissipated; the young manager gets a small amount of seed money $\mu_w p_{t+1}q_{t+1}$, with $\mu_w < 1 - \beta$; and the old manager gets zero. Lenders get the promised repayment L_{t+1} if a bailout is granted and zero otherwise. Since guarantees are systemic, bailouts are paid if and only if many borrowers go bust. For concreteness, we make the following assumption.

Systemic Bailout Guarantees There is a bailout agency that repays lenders 100 percent of what they were promised (L_{t+1}) if a majority of borrowers go bust.[7]

To close the description of the economy, we note that the real ex-change rate is determined by the N-goods market-clearing condition

$$d_t(p_t) + I_t(p_t) = q_t(I_{t-1}). \tag{5.4}$$

Since there are no exogenous shocks, the only source of risk is endogenous real exchange rate variability. As we shall see, there are equilibria where (5.4) holds at two values of p_t: $\bar{p}_{t+1}$ if firms are solvent or $\underline{p}_{t+1}$ if they are insolvent.[8]

Trade and financial liberalization will mean a reduction in im-pediments to trade goods and assets, rather than a shift away from autarky. In a financially nonliberalized economy, there are regula-tions that preclude agents from taking on credit risk that might lead to insolvency. Since the only source of risk is real exchange rate variability, this is equivalent to allowing agents to issue only N debt. Financial liberalization eliminates these regulations, so agents can issue both types of debt. As we shall see, liberalization might lead to currency mismatch and lending booms that end in busts. The effects of trade liberalization are not the focus of the model. Since these reforms typically increase T-sector efficiency, they can be represented by an increase in the productivity parameter a_t in (5.1). To isolate the effects of financial liberalization we will set a_t equal to 1.[9]

Financing and Investment Decisions
Consider first a nonliberalized economy. Since lenders are risk neutral and the opportunity cost of capital is $1 + r$, the interest rate that they require on N-debt (ρ_t^n) satisfies

$$[1 + \rho_t^n]E_t(p_{t+1}) = 1 + r. \tag{5.5}$$

Furthermore, to avoid diversion by the firm, lenders impose the following no-diversion constraint:

$$[1 + r]b_t^n \le h[w_t + b_t^n]. \tag{5.6}$$

This no-diversion condition becomes a borrowing constraint provided the cost of diversion h is greater than the opportunity cost of capital $1 + r$. Otherwise, borrowers would never have an incentive to divert.

   If investment yields a return that is higher than the opportunity cost of capital, the firm will borrow up to an amount that makes the borrowing constraint binding. Thus, budget constraint (5.3) implies that credit and investment are:

$$b_t^n = [m^s - 1]w_t, \quad I_t = m^s \frac{w_t}{p_t}, \quad \text{where } m^s = \frac{1}{1 - h\delta}, \quad \delta \equiv \frac{1}{1 + r}. \tag{5.7}$$

Notice that a necessary condition for borrowing constraints to arise is $h < 1 + r$. If h, the index of contract enforceability, were greater than the cost of capital, it would always be cheaper to repay debt rather than to divert. Hence, lenders will not impose a ceiling on the amount they are willing to lend and agents will not be financially constrained. This is why in the empirical part of this book we differentiate high-h from low-h countries.

Next, consider a liberalized economy. Firms can now choose between N and T debt. If there is enough expected real exchange rate variability (that is, $\underline{p}_{t+1} \ll \bar{p}_{t+1}$), T debt is risky as it might lead to insolvency in the low-price state:

$$\pi(\underline{p}_{t+1}) = \beta \underline{p}_{t+1} q_{t+1} - (1 + \rho_t) b_t < 0,$$

$$\pi(\bar{p}_{t+1}) = \beta \bar{p}_{t+1} q_{t+1} - (1 + \rho_t) b_t \geq 0.$$

A firm might choose T debt and risk insolvency because risky T debt is cheaper than safe N debt. To see why, suppose for a moment that tomorrow's real exchange rate can take on two values. With probability u, it takes an appreciated value ($\bar{p}_{t+1}$) that leaves every firm solvent, while with probability $1 - u$ it takes a depreciated value ($\underline{p}_{t+1}$) that makes all N-sector firms go bust and generates a crisis. Since lenders constrain credit to ensure that borrowers will repay in the no-crisis state, it follows that in the no-crisis state debt is repaid in full and there is no bailout. Meanwhile, in the crisis state there is bankruptcy and each lender receives a bailout equal to what he was promised. Thus, the interest rate on T debt is given by

$$1 + \rho_t = 1 + r, \tag{5.8}$$

while that on N debt is determined by

$$1 + \rho_t^n = \frac{1 + r}{u \bar{p}_{t+1} + (1 - u) \underline{p}_{t+1}}.$$

It follows that choosing T debt over N debt reduces the cost of capital from $1 + r$ to $[1 + r]u$. Lower expected debt repayments, in turn, ease the borrowing constraint as lenders will lend up to an amount that satisfies the following constraint.

$$u[1 + r]b_t \le h[w_t + b_t].\tag{5.9}$$

Comparing borrowing constraint (5.9) with (5.6), we can see that in a risky liberalized economy, agents can borrow more at each level of net worth w_t. Combining (5.8) with (5.9), it follows that in a risky liberalized economy, credit and investment are:

$$b_t = [m^r - 1]w_t, \quad I_t = m^r \frac{w_t}{p_t}, \quad m^r = \frac{1}{1 - u^{-1}h\delta}.\tag{5.10}$$

By comparing (5.10) with (5.7) we can see the following:

Result 1 *In a risky liberalized economy, taking on credit risk allows agents to exploit the subsidy implicit in the systemic bailout guarantees and reduce the expected value of debt repayments. This, in turn, eases borrowing constraints and increases the investment multiplier:* $m^r > m^s$.

This increase in leverage is possible because systemic guarantees mean that in a crisis, lenders expect to be bailed out. Since lenders are competitive, the subsidy implicit in the guarantees is passed on to borrowers.

The fact that T debt is cheaper than N debt does not imply that agents will always be willing to issue T debt. This is because with probability $1 - u$, T debt will result in bankruptcy for a borrower. One can show that it is individually optimal to choose T debt if crises are rare events—that is, u is sufficiently near to 1—and there is enough real exchange rate variability:

$$\frac{\beta\theta\bar{p}_{t+1}}{p_t} \ge \frac{1}{\delta} > h > \frac{\beta\theta\underline{p}_{t+1}}{p_t}.\tag{5.11}$$

The first inequality ensures that in the good state, returns are high enough to make the production of N goods profitable. The third inequality ensures that in the bad state, there is a critical mass of insolvencies so that lenders will be bailed out. Finally, the second inequality is necessary for borrowing constraints to arise in equilibrium.[10]

Equilibria

Here, we investigate when it is that currency mismatch generates price sequences that satisfy (5.11). In the two economies we have considered, investment is given by $I_t = m_t[I_t/p_t]$ and cash flow equals the representative manager's wage: $w_t = [1 - \beta_t]p_t q_t$, where β_t equals β under solvency and μ_w under insolvency. The market-clearing condition (5.4) therefore implies that in any equilibrium

$$I_t = \phi_t q_t, \quad \phi_t = [1 - \beta_t] m_t, \tag{5.12}$$

where the investment multiplier m_t can take the value m^s or m^r. Combining (5.12) with (5.1) and (5.2), we find that in a symmetrical equilibrium, N output, prices, and T output evolve according to

$$q_t = \theta \phi_{t-1} q_{t-1}, \tag{5.13a}$$

$$p_t = \alpha[q_t(1 - \phi_t)]^{\alpha-1}, \tag{5.13b}$$

$$y_t = [q_t(1 - \phi_t)]^\alpha = \frac{1 - \phi_t}{\alpha} p_t q_t. \tag{5.13c}$$

In a nonliberalized economy, the share of N output that the N sector commands for investment purposes is $\phi^s = (1 - \beta)/(1 - h\delta)$ during every period. Thus, there exists an equilibrium in such an economy if and only if: (1) the degree of contract enforceability satisfies $h < \bar{h} = \beta \delta^{-1}$, so that ϕ_t is less than 1; and (2) N sector's productivity satisfies $\theta > \underline{\theta} = [\delta\beta(\phi^s)^{\alpha-1}]^{-1/\alpha}$, so that the production of N goods has a positive net present value $\beta \theta p_{t+1}/p_t \geq \delta^{-1}$.

In a liberalized economy there are two equilibria. We have just characterized the safe one, where agents choose not to issue T debt. There is also a risky equilibrium that is composed of lucky paths that are punctuated by crises. Along a lucky path, all debt is denominated in T goods and lenders will be bailed out in the next period if a majority of firms go bust. Since the debt burden is not indexed to p_t, there are two market-clearing prices. At the high price, firms are solvent and their cash flow is $[1 - \beta]\bar{p}_t q_t$. Thus, $\phi_t = (1 - \beta)m^r$. At the low price, however, N firms are insolvent and their cash flow is only $\mu_w \underline{p}_t q_t$. Moreover, Ranciere, Tornell, and Westermann (2003) show that when $p_t = \underline{p}_t$, leverage is too low for fragility to arise and the real exchange rate to take on two values at $t + 1$. Thus, at the time of the crisis, agents find it optimal to issue N debt and the investment share is $\phi_t = \mu_w m^s$.

Resumption of risk taking takes place in the period after the crisis. Therefore, along a risky equilibrium, the path of N-sector investment is

$$
I_t = \phi_t q_t, \quad \phi_t = \begin{cases} \phi^l = \dfrac{1 - \beta}{1 - u^{-1}h\delta}, & \text{if } p_t = \bar{p}_t, \\[2ex] \phi^c = \dfrac{\mu_w}{1 - h\delta}, & \text{if } p_t = \underline{p}_t. \end{cases} \tag{5.14}
$$

The equilibrium sequence $\{q_t, p_t, y_t\}$ is then determined by using (5.14) to replace ϕ_t in (5.13a) through (5.13b). Ranciere, Tornell, and Westermann (2003) show that if crises are rare events, there are thresholds for the degree of contract enforceability and the N sector's productivity—such that if $h \in (\underline{h}, \bar{h})$ and $\theta \in (\underline{\theta}, \bar{\theta})$, returns satisfy (5.11)—and thus a risky equilibrium exists. Notice that $h < \bar{h}$ and $\theta > \underline{\theta}$ ensure that when crises are rare events, investment is profitable. Meanwhile, $\theta < \bar{\theta}$ and $h > \underline{h}$ ensure that firms with T debt go bust in the bad state, and that the fall in cash flow is translated into a large fall in credit and N investment, so that the fall in prices is validated. This establishes the second result.

Result 2 *Financial liberalization increases investment in the financially constrained sector, but only if agents find it profitable to take on credit risk and the economy becomes financially fragile. This occurs only if contract enforceability problems are severe, but not too severe.*

Two comments are in order. First, notice that no exogenous shocks are necessary for crises; a shift in expectations is sufficient. A crisis can occur whenever each firm expects that others will not undertake credit risk, so that there is a reversion to the safe equilibrium. The key to having multiple market-clearing prices is that part of the N sector's demand comes from the N sector itself. Hence, when the price falls below a cutoff level and N firms go bust, the investment share of the N sector falls (from ϕ^l to ϕ^c). This, in turn, reduces the demand for N goods, validating the fall in the price.

Second, notice that the interaction of contract enforceability problems and systemic guarantees creates the fragility required for self-fulfilling crises. If there were no guarantees, agents would not be willing to take on credit risk to claim the implicit subsidy and currency mismatch would not arise. Costly enforceability of contracts would still imply that the N sector can grow only gradually. Yet there would be no endogenous force that makes a boom end in a crisis. Alternatively, if there were only guarantees but no enforceability problems, then neither borrowing constraints nor balance sheet effects would arise. Thus, N-sector investment would not depend on its cash flow.

An Account of a Boom-Bust Cycle

In this section, we relate the equilibrium time series to the stylized facts of chapter 4. We also discuss what conditions make an economy vulnerable to boom-bust cycles.

Financial liberalization leads to a lending boom and higher GDP growth because it eases the borrowing constraints faced by the N sector. Credit grows fast, but gradually, as borrowing constraints are relaxed only through the reinvestment of profits. In contrast, the T sector does not face financing constraints: its growth is determined by investment opportunities (which in our model grow at a constant rate). This *asymmetry* in the growth patterns of the N and T sectors generates two regularities associated with lending booms: increasing credit-to-GDP and N-to-T output ratios.

If bailout guarantees are present, their interaction with borrowing constraints both fuels the boom and induces endogenous real exchange rate risk. Guarantees alleviate the underinvestment problem usually associated with constrained agents. They permit high leverage with debt denominated in T goods (a currency mismatch) and faster credit growth. As a result, as long as a crisis does not occur, both sectors and GDP grow faster than if guarantees were absent. The currency mismatch nevertheless makes the economy vulnerable to self-fulfilling twin crises where a real depreciation and widespread bankruptcies coincide. Importantly, such crises are not merely financial but have substantial real costs: in the crisis period, cash flow and investment demand collapse. This leads to a credit crunch and a fall in N output. Subsequently, balance sheet effects permit only a slow recovery of N-sector output. Since the T sector is not affected by the credit crunch because it can access international financial markets, there is a decline of the N-to-T output ratio. Furthermore, since domestic credit goes mainly to the N sector, there is a decline in the credit-to-GDP ratio. This provides an account of a complete boom-bust episode.

Who Is to Blame: Bailout Guarantees and Contract Enforceability
A key point is that the *interaction* of contract enforceability problems and systemic bailout guarantees creates the fragility required for self-fulfilling crises. On the one hand, if there were no guaran-

tees, firms would be unwilling to take on insolvency risk. Costly enforceability of contracts would still imply that the N sector can grow only gradually and balance sheet effects could play a role during the lending boom. There would be no force that makes a boom end in a crisis, however. On the other hand, if there were only guarantees but no enforceability problems, borrowing constraints would not arise—a necessary condition for self-fulfilling crises to occur.

There is an interesting *nonlinearity* in the relationship between the degree of contract enforceability (h) and the fragility of the economy. On the one hand, if h were too high, risky equilibria would not exist. In this case, at the level of the individual firm, a credit constraint would not arise. Balance sheet effects are then absent and crises cannot occur. In other words, our crisis mechanism cannot work in countries where there are no asymmetries in financing opportunities and the N sector is well integrated into international credit markets. On the other hand, if h is quite small, balance sheet effects are not strong enough. This precludes the existence of lending booms. Obviously, countries in which banks have little access to international credit markets should not be expected to exhibit lending booms and are therefore also immune to crises.

How Likely Is a Crisis?

The model implies that the likelihood of a self-fulfilling crisis is not a free parameter. If crises were not rare events, the production of N goods would not be a positive net present-value undertaking. This implies that an equilibrium with binding borrowing constraints would not exist. In other words, self-fulfilling crises must be rare in order to occur in equilibrium.

GDP Growth and Financial Fragility

In this section, we establish the link between GDP growth and fragility. Since N goods are intermediate inputs while T goods are

final-consumption goods, GDP equals the value of N-sector investment plus T output: $gdp_t = p_t I_t + y_t$. It then follows from (5.12)
through (5.13c) that

$$gdp_t = y_t + p_t \phi_t q_t = q_t^\alpha Z(\phi_t) = y_t \frac{Z(\phi_t)}{[1 - \phi_t]}, \quad Z(\phi_t) = \frac{1 - [1 - \alpha]\phi_t}{[1 - \phi_t]^{1-\alpha}}$$

(5.15)

As we can see, the key determinants of the evolution of GDP are
the technological coefficient in T production (a_t) and the share of N
output invested by the N sector (ϕ_t). In order to isolate the effects of
financial liberalization, we have set a_t equal to 1.

In a nonliberalized economy, the investment share ϕ_t is constant
and equal to ϕ^s. Thus, GDP and T output grow at a common rate:

$$1 + \gamma^{NL} := \frac{gdp_t}{gdp_{t-1}} = \frac{y_t}{y_{t-1}} = (\theta \phi^s)^\alpha.$$

(5.16)

Absent technological progress in the T sector, N-sector growth is
the force driving growth in both sectors. As the N sector expands,
N goods become more abundant and cheaper, allowing the T sector
to expand production. This expansion is possible if and only if N-
sector productivity (θ) and the share of N output reinvested by the
N sector (ϕ^s) are high enough, so that credit and N output can grow
over time: $B_t / B_{t-1} = q_t / q_{t-1} = \theta \phi^s > 1$.[11] As we can see, if the degree of contract enforceability h is small, the N-sector investment
share will also be small. GDP growth will be low as a consequence.

Let us now consider a liberalized economy. Along a risky equilibrium of such an economy, there is a succession of lucky paths punctuated by crisis episodes. An economy is on a lucky path at time t if
there was no crisis either at $t - 1$ or t. Since along a lucky path the
investment share equals ϕ^l, (5.15) implies that the common growth
rate of GDP and T output is

$$1 + \gamma^L = (\theta \phi^l)^\alpha.$$

(5.17)

A comparison of γ^L and γ^{NL} reveals that as long as a crisis does not occur, growth in a liberalized economy is greater than in a nonliberalized one. In the presence of systemic guarantees, credit risk allows financially constrained N firms to borrow and invest more than in a nonliberalized economy $(\phi^l > \phi^s)$. Since there are sectoral linkages $(\alpha > 0)$, this increase in the N sector's investment share benefits both the T and N sectors.

Because self-fulfilling crises occur with probability $1 - u$, and during a crisis the investment share falls from ϕ^l to $\phi^c < \phi^s$, the fact that $\gamma^L > \gamma^{NL}$ does not imply that financial liberalization necessarily leads to higher mean GDP growth. The reduction in the investment share comes about through two channels: (1) N-sector firms go bust and their cash flow collapses (captured by $\mu_w/(1 - \beta)$), and (2) leverage falls because firms cannot take on credit risk (indexed by $(1 - h\delta)/(1 - h\delta u^{-1})$). It follows from (5.15) that in a crisis episode that lasts two periods, the mean crisis growth rate is

$$1 + \gamma^{cr} = \theta^\alpha (\phi^l \phi^c)^{\alpha/2}. \tag{5.18}$$

As we can see, variations in GDP growth generated by real exchange rate changes at τ and $\tau + 1$ cancel out. Thus, the average loss in GDP growth stems only from the fall in the N sector's average investment share.

A liberalized economy experiences several crises over time. Therefore, to see whether financial liberalization will increase average long-run growth, one needs to compute the limit distribution of GDP's growth rate. Ranciere, Tornell, and Westermann (2003) show that (5.17) and (5.18) imply that over the long run, the mean compounded growth rate of the GDP in a liberalized economy is

$$E(1 + \gamma^L) = (1 + \gamma^l)^\omega (1 + \gamma^{cr})^{1-\omega}$$

$$= \theta^\alpha (\phi^l)^{\alpha\omega} (\phi^l \phi^c)^{\alpha((1-\omega)/2)}, \quad \text{where } \omega = \frac{u}{2 - u}. \tag{5.19}$$

Notice that ω is the proportion of time that the economy is on a lucky path over the long run. A comparison of long-run GDP growth rates in (5.16) and (5.19) reveals the following:

Result 3   *Average long-run GDP growth is greater in a liberalized economy than in a nonliberalized one provided that contract enforceability problems are severe, but not too severe, and that financial distress during crises is not too large.*

This result means that except for a few unlucky risky paths, most of the risky paths will outperform the safe path over the long run. Of course, for a given realization of the sunspot process, it is possible that in the short run, GDP growth will be greater along a safe path. This is because many crises are concentrated in the short run. Over the long run, however, the crisis-prone liberalized economy will, on average, overtake the safe economy.

The relationship between financial liberalization and growth is not straightforward because an increase in the probability of crisis $(1 - u)$ has ambiguous effects on long-run growth. On the one hand, a greater $1 - u$ increases investment and growth along the lucky path by increasing the subsidy implicit in the guarantee and allowing N-sector firms to be more leveraged. On the other hand, a greater $1 - u$ makes crises more frequent. The degree of contract enforceability (h) plays a key role. If we increase $1 - u$, the growth-enhancing effect of more investment dominates the growth-reducing effect of more frequent crises when h is large enough. This is because a large h increases firms' leverage and allows them to reap the benefits of risk taking. Yet h cannot be arbitrarily large to ensure the existence of an equilibrium. If h were extremely large, borrowing constraints would not arise (by [5.10]) or there would not be market clearing, as $\phi^l > 1$ (by [5.14]).

The central role played by the requirement that "h must be low, but not too low" underlies the importance of the country sample

over which the empirical link between liberalization and growth
exists. The above result implies that among the set of countries
where contract enforceability problems are severe, but not too
severe, financial liberalization may lead to higher growth even if
we control for trade liberalization. This prediction establishes a
causal link from liberalization to GDP growth in the regressions of
chapter 3.

Credit Growth
Here, we sketch the argument used by Ranciere, Tornell, and Westermann (2003) to show that economies that have followed growth-
enhancing risky credit paths are identified by a negatively skewed
distribution of credit growth. Since in the model N firms use only
N inputs, the appropriate measure of real credit is $\tilde{b}_t = (b_t + b_t^n)/p_t$.
It follows from (5.7) and (5.10) that in a risky and safe economy,
real credit is given, respectively, by

$$\tilde{b}_t^{LE} = \begin{cases} [\phi^l - (1-\beta)]q_t, & \text{if } \pi(p_t) \geq 0, \\ [\phi^c - \mu_w]q_t, & \text{if } \pi(p_t) < 0, \end{cases} \qquad \tilde{b}_t^{NL} = [\phi^s - (1-\beta)]q_t.$$

$$(5.20)$$

In a safe nonliberalized economy credit follows a smooth path,
while in a risky liberalized economy it follows a bumpy path. Using
(5.13a), we find that in the latter, the compounded growth rate of
credit is $\zeta^l = \log(\theta\phi^l)$ along a lucky path, $\zeta^c = \log(\theta\phi^l u(\mu_w/(1-\beta)) \cdot ((1-h\delta u^{-1})/(1-h\delta)))$ during a crisis, and $\zeta^p = \log(\theta\phi^l(1/u))$ in the
postcrisis period.

When skewness is negative, the good outcomes in the distribution lie closer to the mean than do the bad outcomes. We find this
credit pattern in the risky equilibrium because N firms face endogenous borrowing constraints, so N-sector credit is constrained by
cash flow. Along the lucky path—in which no crises occur—cash
flow accumulates gradually and credit can grow only gradually. In
contrast, when a crisis erupts there are widespread bankruptcies

and cash flow collapses. Credit growth thus falls sharply ($\zeta^c < \zeta^l$). In the wake of a crisis, credit growth rebounds before returning to its lucky level ($\zeta^p > \zeta^l$). As long as crises are rare events, the credit growth rates during the postcrisis period and the lucky path are close, ($\zeta^p - \zeta^l$) = $\log(u^{-1})$. Ranciere, Tornell, and Westermann (2003) show that since falls and rebounds occur with the same frequency, the distribution of credit growth is characterized by negative outliers in a long enough sample.

Result 4   *In a risky liberalized economy, the limit distribution of credit growth has negative skewness. Meanwhile, in a nonliberalized economy, credit growth has a smooth path with zero skewness.*

To link this result to our empirical findings, recall that a risky equilibrium exists only if enforceability problems are severe, but not too severe—a condition we find in MICs. The first implication of this result is that financial liberalization may lead to bumpiness of credit growth across MICs. Since negative skewness of credit growth implies the adoption of credit risk, which eases financial constraints and leads to an increase in mean GDP growth (per result three), the second implication is that negative skewness is an appropriate right-hand-side variable in the growth regressions we estimate.

Notice that if enforceability problems were either not severe or too severe, there would be no endogenous force that would make credit growth negatively skewed to begin with. As such, the link between negative skewness and growth would not exist. This is why skewness is statistically significant in all growth regressions, even if we do not condition on the sample of countries.

In the model, credit growth exhibits more variance in the liberalized economy. Empirically, though, variance is not a good means of identifying economies that have followed growth-enhancing risky credit paths that lead to infrequent crises. High variance is not only generated by occasional crises but may also be generated by high-frequency shocks, which might be exogenous or self-inflicted by, for instance, procyclic fiscal policy. To generate high variance in both the safe and risky equilibria, one could include in the model high-frequency exogenous shocks that do not lead to crises. Such shocks would increase the variance of credit growth in both econo-mies, but would not increase mean GDP growth. The two equilib-riums would still be distinguished by negative skewness of credit growth because only the risky equilibrium would be crisis prone.

The N-to-T Output Ratio

We have captured the sectoral asymmetry in financing opportuni-ties prevalent in MICs by assuming that T production is not affected by financial constraints, while the N sector faces contract enforce-ability problems. This sectoral asymmetry generates two predic-tions about the behavior of the N-to-T output ratio (N/T) that help us identify the mechanism that links liberalization, fragility, and growth in MICs.

Since the N sector is more financially constrained than the T sec-tor, the first prediction is that along any equilibrium path, N/T is positively correlated with domestic credit growth. To derive the second prediction, note that it follows from (5.13a) through (5.13c) that in a symmetrical equilibrium, N/T is given by

$$\frac{N_t}{T_t} \equiv \frac{p_t q_t}{y_t} = \frac{p_t q_t}{((1 - \phi_t)/\alpha)p_t q_t} = \frac{\alpha}{1 - \phi_t}. \tag{5.21}$$

Investment equations (5.7) and (5.10) imply that when there is a shift from a nonliberalized to a liberalized economy, the N-to-T output ratio increases from $\alpha/(1 - \phi^s)$ to $\alpha/(1 - \phi^l)$. This reflects the fact that financial liberalization eases financial constraints and allows the N sector to command a greater share of N inputs.[12]

If a crisis occurs at some date, say τ, there is a *fire sale*: there is a steep real exchange rate depreciation, and since there is currency mismatch, all N firms default. As a result, the investment share falls from ϕ^l to ϕ^c. The price of N goods must fall to allow the T sector to absorb a greater share of N output, which is predetermined by $\tau - 1$ investment. As we can see in (5.21), N/T falls from $\alpha/(1 - \phi^l)$ to $\alpha/(1 - \phi^c)$. Thus,

Result 5 *Across MICs, the N-to-T output ratio (1) responds positively to financial liberalization and negatively to crises, and (2) is positively correlated with credit growth.*

Both of these implications of sectorial asymmetries are consistent with the stylized facts we documented in chapters 3 and 4. Furthermore, sectorial asymmetries are key to explaining several features of the boom-bust cycles experienced by many MICs.

Production Efficiency and Welfare

We have considered an endogenous growth model whereby the financially constrained N sector is the engine of growth because it produces the intermediate input used throughout the economy. Thus, the share of N output invested in the N sector, φ_t, is the critical determinant of economic growth. When φ_t is too small, T output is high in the short run, but long-run growth is slow. In contrast, when φ_t is too high, there is an inefficient accumulation of N goods. It follows that in order to determine whether financial liberalization improves welfare despite the occurrence of crises, one needs to determine whether there is a bottleneck—that is, whether the share sequence (φ_t) is too low. Then one needs to determine the conditions under which social welfare is higher in a liberalized economy, where agents undertake credit risk and crises can occur.

These issues are addressed by Ranciere, Tornell, and Westermann (2003). They show that if the degree of contract enforceability h is below a certain threshold, then in a nonliberalized economy the N sector investment share φ_t is below the Pareto optimal level (that is, there is a bottleneck). They also show that, by allowing agents to take on credit risk, financial liberalization leads to an increase in the average share φ_t. This brings the allocation nearer to the Pareto optimal allocation, increasing the present value of T output. Moreover, if there is a bottleneck, crises are rare events, and the costs of crises are not too high, then ex ante social welfare in a liberalized economy is greater than in a nonliberalized economy even if bailout costs are funded via domestic taxation.

Recall that in a liberalized economy credit risk makes the economy vulnerable to crises, which entail costs for the economy. The question then arises as to whether it is worthwhile to incur the crisis costs in order to attain higher growth. A crisis involves two deadweight losses for the economy as a whole: the revenues dissipated in bankruptcy procedures and the fall in N-sector investment due to its weakened financial position. Thus, if crises entail small bankruptcy costs and mild financial distress costs, the only first-order effect of a crisis is to reduce transitorily the N sector's investment share. Therefore, if there is a bottleneck and crises are rare events, the greater average investment share will increase the present value of T output and hence welfare.

We have seen that the undertaking of credit risk is supported by bailout guarantees. Since these guarantees are funded by domestic taxation, the question arises as to whether consumers will be willing to foot the tax bill.

Credit risk eases borrowing constraints and leads to a greater mean growth of N output even if crises do occur. As a result, T production will enjoy cheaper and more abundant N inputs, and its mean growth rate will also increase. This benefits consumers because they receive a share $1 - \alpha$ of T output as income. Since the representative consumer has access to complete capital markets, that individual can perfectly smooth the cost of the guarantees. Following this logic, Ranciere, Tornell, and Westermann (2003) show that when social welfare gains are present, consumer welfare gains are also present if the share $1 - \alpha$ is large enough.

The funding of the guarantees by consumers operates a redistribution from the nonconstrained T sector to the constrained N sector. Such a redistribution is to the mutual benefit of both sectors. It is a Pareto-improving policy.

Literature Review

Several ingredients of the argument presented above have been examined previously in the literature. The papers on which this chapter is based synthesize several elements of the existing literature. To our knowledge, this synthesis is the first attempt to formally rationalize a complete boom-bust cycle as well as to formally study bailout guarantees and a contract enforceability problem in a unified framework in order to develop a growth model where crises can occur, and where the trade-off between growth and macroeconomic risk can be evaluated.

Beginning with Bernanke and Gertler (1989) as well as Kiyotaki and Moore (1997), balance sheet effects have been at the heart of a large literature in macroeconomics.[13] Recent applications in a two-sector, open economy context include Aghion, Bachetta, and Banerjee (2000) along with Caballero and Krishnamurthy (2001). In Aghion, Bachetta, and Banerjee (2000), T goods are produced using a country-specific factor, which is nontradable. In their setup, it is the T sector that is constrained by net worth and there are no bailout guarantees. An increase in T-sector net worth has two effects. First, it relaxes borrowing constraints, increasing investment and future net worth. Second, if the supply of the N input is sufficiently inelastic, it drives up the input's price. As T-sector wealth builds up, the second effect gains strength. Thus, there is a time when the real appreciation spell comes to an end and there is a drastic real depreciation. Like the present chapter's model, this model derives endogenous volatility from balance sheet effects. Caballero and Krishnamurthy (2001) consider a three-period, two-sector economy with credit constraints. As we do, they single out the N sector as having more difficulties in obtaining external finance. They do so by assuming that it cannot borrow directly from abroad. This creates a distinction between an economy's international collateral and domestic collateral, provided by the T sector and domestic collateral, which the N sector needs for borrowing from the T sector. They show that N-sector firms do not have incentives to hedge and that in a crisis, shocks can get propagated across sectors and amplified through collateral prices. In contrast to our story, exogenous shocks are essential for crises to occur. Moreover, the model is not designed to generate a boom-bust cycle as it is essentially static.

Bailout guarantees have been prominent in discussions of the Asian crisis. Corsetti, Pesenti, and Roubini (1999), Krugman (1999), and McKinnon and Pill (1997) all emphasize the role of guarantees for overinvestment and the behavior of asset prices. Burnside, Eichenbaum, and Rebelo (2001) show that bailout guarantees discourage agents from hedging their foreign currency exposure. In their model, banks borrow in foreign currency and lend in domestic currency. Self-fulfilling devaluations are possible because a devaluation transforms government's contingent liabilities into actual liabilities and depletes government reserves. Their model is not designed to fit the other regularities associated with the boom-bust cycle because it does not give rise to credit constraints and it considers a one-sector economy.

In terms of the "crisis mechanism," the papers most related to this chapter are Calvo (1998) and Krugman (1999). They also argue that with risky debt denomination, balance sheet effects can be responsible for self-fulfilling meltdowns. In contrast this chapter, they simply assume the existence of foreign currency–denominated debt and credit constraints.

Following Obstfeld (1986), a number of other papers have described crises in models with multiple equilibria. Cole and Kehoe (2000) stress coordination problems among lenders in the presence of short-term debt. Chang and Velasco (1998) consider a similar setup where banks play a key role. In these models, lenders refuse to roll over debt because they fear others may also refuse to do so. Although this coordination failure can also occur in our model, it is distinct from the self-fulfilling real depreciations we emphasize here. A model based only on coordination failure cannot account for the protracted credit crunches and declining credit-to-deposits ratios observed in the aftermath of crises.

There are no banks in the model presented in this chapter. The credit chain is subsumed in a single borrower-lender relationship. Holmstrom and Tirole (1997) and Tirole (2002) have modeled how the capital of the banking system constrains lending, and hence spills over to bank-dependent firms and constrains their investment. The role of banks in the spread of crises has been analyzed by Diamond and Rajan (2000). Enforceability problems imply that the only way illiquid investments can be financed is through domestic banks, which in turn must borrow short-term. A crisis occurs when an exogenous productivity shock forces early liquidation. This precipitates a meltdown of the banking sector and generates a credit crunch.

The link between growth and crises that we emphasize in this book is reminiscent of the literature on risk as a factor of production as Sinn (1986) and Konrad (1992).

In HICs, it is often debated whether governments should support a higher degree of risk taking in the economy—for instance, by subsidizing venture capital firms. In the absence of the credit market imperfections that are characteristic of MICs, the arguments in this book do not support these kind of policies.

6   Credit Market Imperfections in Middle-Income Countries

In this chapter, we use macro- and microlevel data to document three credit market imperfections—asymmetrical financing opportunities, currency mismatch, and systemic guarantees—that are prevalent in MICs and underlie the mechanism we modeled in chapter 5.

The boom-bust cycles and other macroeconomic patterns we have documented in earlier chapters are not observed in countries with developed financial markets. They appear to be the same across MICs, in spite of different exchange rate regimes. These facts indicate that the mechanisms at work are not dependent on particular features of the nominal regime but rather on other institutional characteristics of MICs.

We have argued in chapter 3 that many MIC macroeconomic patterns are generated by the interaction of three characteristics of financing typical of MICs. The first of these is that although borrowing constraints affect many firms in MICs, the incidence of these constraints is heavily biased toward the N sector—a fact that is key to explaining the MIC macroeconomic patterns. While T-sector firms tend to be large and have access to world capital markets, N-sector firms are smaller on average and are bank dependent. That is, there is a pronounced sectoral asymmetry in financing opportunities.[1]

Second, in MICs a substantial amount of N-sector debt is dollar denominated, while the income streams that service those debts are in domestic currency. Since domestic banks are heavily exposed to the N sector, the degree of currency mismatch is significant. Even when the banks' balance sheets are equilibrated, banks face a de facto currency mismatch because they lend primarily to the N sector. Thus, they face insolvency risk.

The prevalence of currency mismatch does not appear out of the blue but rather is the optimal response of borrowers and creditors to the existence of systemic bailout guarantees—the third imperfection we document here. In MICs as well as many other countries, creditors are covered, either explicitly or implicitly, by systemic bailout guarantees. It is expected that if a critical mass of debtors risks insolvency, the government will implement policies to ensure that the creditors are repaid (at least in part), thereby averting an economic meltdown. These policies may come in the form of an easing of monetary policy, the maintenance of an exchange rate peg, or the handing out of checks.

Asymmetrical Financing Opportunities

In order to investigate the existence of sectoral asymmetries in financing opportunities, we use three microlevel data sets: the *World Business Economic Survey* (*WBES*) of the World Bank; the Mexican economic census; and the firms listed on the Mexican stock exchange (Bolsa Mexicana de Valores, or BMV). The *WBES* consists of a panel of 3,777 firms, covering twenty-six countries out of our MIC sample.[2] The BMV set contains the Mexican firms that issue either bonds or equity (310 firms), whereas the Mexican census includes all firms in Mexico (2,788,222 firms). Furthermore, we show that capital flows in the form of FDI mostly go to the tradable sector.

Evidence from the *WBES*
This survey classifies firms according to their size and, among other things, whether they export. Since the share of T output in the

Table 6.1
Sectorial and size distributions in MICs

	N sector (percent)	T sector (percent)
Small	68	32
Large	33	67

group of export firms is greater than that of nonexport firms, we identify exporters with T-sector firms and nonexporters with N-sector firms.

The first question we ask is whether firms in the T sector tend to be larger than those in the N sector. The answer is positive. Table 6.1 shows that across the twenty-six countries in the *WBES* survey, a majority (68 percent) of small and medium firms belong to the N sector, while a majority (67 percent) of large firms belong to the T sector. There are some large firms in the N sector, such as utilities and telecommunications firms; however, these large N-sector firms do not represent a large share of firms in the survey.

Table 6.2 shows that most MICs exhibit the same distribution of firms as the distribution of the aggregate, depicted in table 6.1.

The survey also asked firms to rank, on a scale from one to four, how much of an obstacle financing presented to running their business. We use the answers from this survey to estimate an ordered probit model to assess whether there exists an asymmetry in financing opportunities across the N and T sectors.[3]

We create a "nonexport" dummy variable for the yes-or-no answer to the question "Do you export?" The dummy takes the value of one if the firm does not export and 0 otherwise. A significant positive parameter on the dummy indicates that N-sector firms evaluate the access to finance as a significantly larger obstacle to running their business than do T-sector firms. We estimate ordered probit regressions of the following form:

$$y_i^* = \beta_0 + \beta_1 NONEXP + \gamma_1 d_1 + \cdots + \gamma_n d_n + \varepsilon_i, \tag{6.1}$$

$$y_i^* = \beta_0 + \beta_1(1 - NONEXP) * EXPSHARE$$

$$+ \gamma_1 d_1 + \cdots + \gamma_n d_n + \varepsilon_i, \tag{6.2}$$

$$y_i^* = \beta_0 + \beta_1 NONEXP * L + \beta_2 NONEXP * S$$

$$+ \beta_3 AGE + \beta_4 GOV + \gamma_1 d_1 + \cdots + \gamma_n d_n + \varepsilon_i, \tag{6.3}$$

$$\text{where} \quad y_i = \begin{cases} 1 & if & y_i^* < \alpha_1 \\ 2 & if & \alpha_1 < y_i^* < \alpha_2 \\ 3 & if & \alpha_2 < y_i^* < \alpha_3 \\ 4 & if & \alpha_3 < y_i^* \end{cases},$$

$n \in \{9, 26\}$, and NONEXP is a dummy that takes the value of one, if the firm does not export. EXPSHARE is the share of exports in output among exporting firms. GOV controls for government participation in the firm, AGE denotes the year a firm was established, and $d_1 \ldots d_n$ are country dummies. L and S denote large and small firms. The dependent variable, y, captures the ranking of the severity of an obstacle for running a business, as perceived by the firms. The obstacles considered are financing, collateral, and the exchange rate. The true y is not directly observed and the "α" parameters are estimated together with $\beta_0 \ldots \beta_3$ and $\gamma_1 \ldots \gamma_n$.

Table 6.3 reports the regression results: regression 1 is the basic regression where we regress the perceived credit constraints on the nonexport dummy. Regression 2 replaces the nonexport dummy by a variable that measures the percentage of output that is exported by exporters. Regression 3 reports the results of a regression that differentiates between small and large N firms, and includes the age of the firm and the share of government participation as control variables.

In all regressions, we find that there is a significant difference between exporters and nonexporters in their evaluations of financ-

Table 6.2
Sectorial and size distributions for individual countries

	N sector (percent)	T sector (percent)
Argentina		
Small	74	26
Large	67	33
Brazil		
Small	73	27
Large	60	40
Chile		
Small	63	37
Large	48	52
Indonesia		
Small	82	18
Large	54	46
Malaysia		
Small	65	35
Large	40	60
Mexico		
Small	68	32
Large	38	62
Philippines		
Small	73	27
Large	48	52
Thailand		
Small	61	39
Large	24	76

Notes: "Small" denotes small and medium firms up to two hundred employees. "Large" firms have more than two hundred employees.
Source: World Business Environment Survey, 2001.

Table 6.3
Asymmetrical financing opportunities

Dependent variable: The answer to the question,
"Is financing a major obstacle to running your business?"

	1	2	3
nonexport	0.303*** (0.064)		
[1 − nonexport] * Share		−0.003*** (0.001)	
nonexport * Large			0.447*** (0.084)
nonexport * Share			0.166** (0.087)
Age			−0.000 (0.002)
Government share			−0.004*** (0.001)

Notes: The table reports regression results of ordered probit regressions, specified with a constant and country dummies. The answer to the question, "Is financing a major obstacle to running your business?" is evaluated on a scale from one to four. Standard errors are reported in parentheses; *indicates significance at the 10 percent level, **indicates significance at the 5 percent level, and ***indicates significance at the 1 percent level.

ing as an obstacle to running their businesses. The latter consider the obstacle to be more severe. Furthermore, we find that among exporters, the larger the share of exports in output, the less significant is financing deemed to be as an obstacle for running a business. We also find that older firms have easier access to financing than younger ones do. The same is true for firms with high government participation. None of the control variables, however, obviates the role of the exporters/nonexporters indicator.

Next, we ask whether bank credit depends on collateral, and whether there is a statistically significant difference between the N and T sectors in this respect. Tables 6.4 and 6.5 shed light on this question. Table 6.4 shows that in most MICs, the majority of bank

Table 6.4
The use of collateral in securing loans

Indonesia	50–60%
Korea	90%
Malaysia	40%
Philipines	50–60%
Thailand	50–60%

Source: D. Dwor-Frecaut, M. Hallward-Driemeier, and F. X. Colaço, "Asian Corporates' Credit Need and Governance" (paper presented at the World Bank conference, Bankok, 1999).

Table 6.5
The role of collateral as an obstacle to obtain financing

Dependent variable: The answer to the question,
"Is collateral a major obstacle to obtain financing?"

	1	2	3
N-sector firms	0.203***		
	(0.062)		
Share of exports		−0.0005*	
		(0.008)	
NL			0.119*
			(0.085)
NS			0.052*
			(0.089)
Age			−0.005**
			(0.001)
Government share			−0.001
			(0.001)

Notes: The table reports regression results of ordered probit regressions, specified with a constant and country dummies. The answer to the question, "Is collateral a major obstacle to obtain financing?" is evaluated on a scale from one to four. The independent variable in regression 1 is a dummy that is equal to one for N-sector firms and zero otherwise. In regression 2, it is the share of exports among T-sector firms. In regression 3, NL = nontradable and large, and NS = nontradable and small; also noted is the age of the firm as well as the share of government participation. Standard errors are reported in parentheses; *indicates significance at the 10 percent level, **indicates significance at the 5 percent level, and ***indicates significance at the 1 percent level.

Table 6.6
Structure of corporate financing in Korea

	1997	1998	1999
Borrowing from domestic money banks			
Large	25	29.6	28.1
Small and medium	74.8	70.3	71.8
Gross issuance of corporate bonds			
Large	90.8	99.1	94.3
Small and medium	9.2	0.9	5.7

Source: International Monetary Fund Country Report 00/10.

loans are indeed secured by collateral. The amount ranges from 40 percent in Malaysia to 90 percent in Korea. In table 6.5, we again make use of the *WBES* data set, where firms were also asked to evaluate how much of an obstacle the access to collateral presents to running their business. Table 6.5 shows that even after controlling for other factors, such as government share and the age of the firm, the importance of collateral is viewed as significantly more severe by the firms in the N sector than those in the T sector.

Aside from easier access to bank credit, firms in the T sector typically are large firms that have the possibility to issue bonds and stocks as substitutes for bank credit. Figure 6.6 illustrates this for the case of Korea. While small and medium enterprises account for about 75 percent of domestic bank credit, more than 90 percent of domestic bonds were issued by large firms.

FDI Is Allocated Mostly to the T Sector

During the last two decades, capital inflows to MICs have increased enormously, and so has the importance of private flows (figures 6.1 and 6.2). In the average MIC the share of private flows increased from 60 percent in the mid-1980s to more than 90 percent by the end of the 1990s.

A. MICs

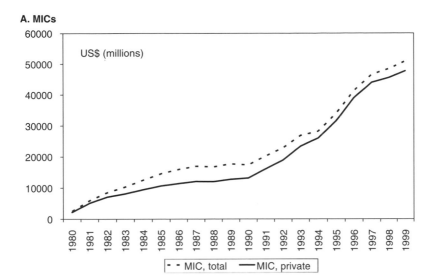

B. Mexico

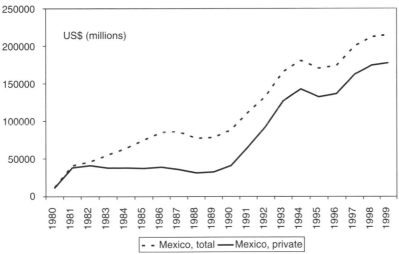

Figure 6.1
Capital inflows
Note: The figures show the total accumulated financial inflows in US$ (millions).
Source: International Monetary Fund, International Financial Statistics.

A. MICs

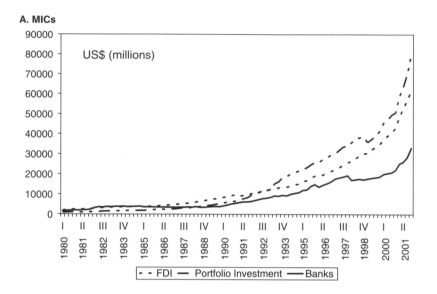

B. Mexico

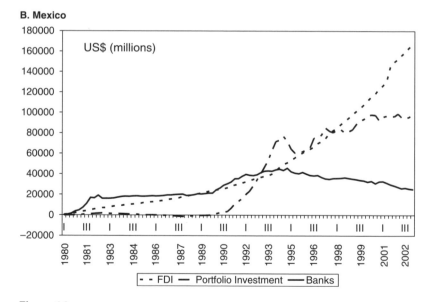

Figure 6.2
Components of private capital inflows
Note: Banks include commercial and development banks.
Sources: IFS, IMF, and Bank of Mexico.

Table 6.7
FDI originating in the United States in 1998

	N	T	F
All countries	0.260	0.275	0.465
HICs	0.260	0.232	0.508
MICs	0.265	0.416	0.319
Mexico	0.154	0.592	0.255

Source: Bureau of Economic Analysis.

FDI is often considered a "good" form of capital inflow, whereas bank flows are considered "bad" because they are foreign loans to domestic banks. Such loans are risky because of the currency mismatch.

Several observers have noted that one reason why financial liberalization has led to financial fragility is that an important share of capital inflows takes the form of bank flows. Many have argued that the greater the share of inflows in the form of FDI and the lower the share of bank credit, the lower the financial fragility.

To evaluate this argument we must keep in mind a further key fact overlooked by the literature: the lion's share of FDI is directed mostly to the T sector or to financial institutions, which we illustrate in table 6.7. Because the nonfinancial N sector receives a small share of FDI, bank flows remain the main source of external finance for most N-sector firms. Since this group of firms is financially constrained, a reduction in risky bank flows and credit may mean that N-sector investment and growth will fall. As there are productive linkages throughout the economy, the unconstrained T sector will also be negatively affected. Hence, it is possible that the net effect of banning risky bank flows is to reduce long-run GDP growth. Here again we see that, in the presence of credit market imperfections, a policy that reduces financial fragility can, as a by-product, lead to a fall in growth.[4]

Table 6.8
Mexican firms in the T and N sectors by firm size, 1999

	Economic census					
	Number of firms		Share of sector sales (percent)		BMV-listed firms (number)	
	N	T	N	T	N	T
Small	2,371,468	329,242	56	10	0	0
Medium	65,630	12,054	32	26	0	0
Large	4,239	5,589	12	64	110	200

Notes: Size is defined in terms of fixed assets in thousands of 1994 U.S. dollars. Categories are: small < $148, medium < $2,370, and large > $2,371. T sectors include primary sectors and manufacturing. N sectors include construction, trade, telecom, transportation, hotels and restaurants, real estate, and other services. Excluded sectors are financial services, electricity, gas, and water. For those firms entering between 2000 and 2002, or exiting between 1991 and 1999, we took the year closest to 1999 for which data on total assets was available for the firms.

Sectoral Asymmetries in Mexico: What Do Microlevel Data Say?

We will analyze two Mexican data sets.[5] The first consists of data on firms listed on the BMV and the second is the economic census. We will see that parallel to the *WBES* findings, T-sector firms in Mexico are, on average, larger than N-sector ones and have better access to international financial markets. We will also show that in the aftermath of the Tequila crisis, T-sector firms were not as hard-hit by the credit crunch as N-sector firms.

The BMV set contains only large firms, whereas the vast majority of firms in the economy are small and medium size (see table 6.8). Moreover, although the BMV set contains both N- and T-sector firms, it is more representative of the T sector than the N sector. The bias is greater for the N sector than for the T sector, both in terms of the distribution of fixed assets (figure 6.3) and in terms of sales. For instance, as table 6.8 also shows, the sales of large N-sector firms constitute only 12 percent of economy-wide N-sector sales, according to the census of 1999, whereas the corresponding

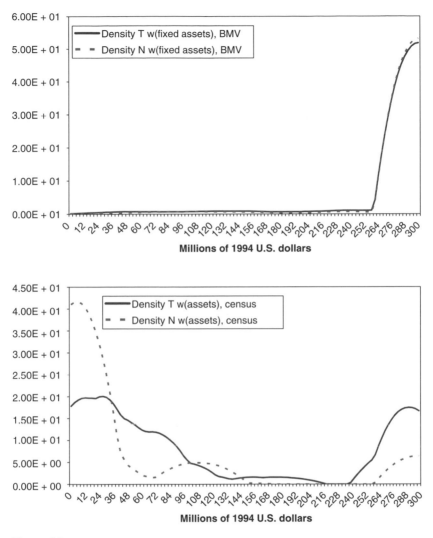

Figure 6.3
The stock market is not representative of the economy

Table 6.9
Issuance of long-term bonds and equity

Year	Total (percent)	Long-term debt (percent)	Equity (percent)
1991	0.9	0.5	0.4
1992	2.0	1.7	0.2
1993	2.2	2.0	0.2
1994	1.3	1.1	0.1
1995	0.5	0.5	—
1996	3.8	3.8	—
1997	5.8	5.0	0.7
1998	3.0	3.0	—
1999	1.4	1.1	0.3
2000	3.2	3.1	0.0
2001	2.0	2.0	—

Issuance/long-term liabilities and equity

Notes: Total gross issuance of long-term corporate bonds (maturity of one year or longer) and equity over the stock of outstanding long-term liabilities plus the stock of equity. Average of all nonfinancial firms that were listed on the BMV throughout the period 1990–2000, and for which there were balance sheet data available.

share for large T-sector firms is 64 percent (excluding financial firms in both cases).

Because the BMV set is biased toward the T sector, and firms in this set are the only ones that issue bonds and equity internationally, it follows that the T sector has better access than the N sector to international financial markets. To the extent that Mexico is typical of other MICs, this fact provides an important warning. In contrast to HICs, in MICs stock market–based data sets (such as *Datastream* or *Worldscope*) do not reflect economy-wide behavior but rather are biased toward the T sector.

To get an idea of the extent to which the crisis affected the access of BMV firms to external financing, consider the ratio of issuance of long-term bonds and equity to the stock of bonds and equity. Table

Table 6.10
Entry and exit from the BMV

	Entries/listed firms (percent)	Exits/listed firms (percent)
1990	3.6	0.0
1991	16.4	1.7
1992	7.5	12.0
1993	10.2	3.9
1994	11.1	6.7
1995	2.1	6.4
1996	8.1	3.0
1997	11.2	3.5
1998	1.9	5.8
1999	0.7	1.4
2000	2.7	2.1
2001	0.7	3.4
2002	2.2	0.0

Notes: Entries are defined as the number of new firms listed on the BMV. Exits are defined as the firms that left the stock market or were suspended in a given year, and were still suspended in 2003. The number of listed companies includes public firms plus some private firms that had issued corporate bonds.

6.9 shows that this ratio jumped from an average of 1.6 percent in 1991–1994 to 4.7 percent in 1996–1997.[6] This jump indicates that BMV firms were not hard-hit by the credit crunch.

Another fact that points in the same direction is that there was no significant increase in bankruptcies among BMV firms. As table 6.10 shows, 6 percent of firms exited the BMV in 1995, and 3 percent in 1996. The average rate of exit over the entire sample period was 3.6 percent, with a standard deviation of 3.5 percent. The increase in bankruptcies in 1995 was therefore not statistically significant.

The availability of external finance for the BMV firms contrasts with the protracted fall in the nationwide credit-to-GDP ratio over 1995–2001. The reason is that the BMV firms shifted away from domestic bank credit in the wake of the crisis. This shift is reflected in

Table 6.11
Shift away from domestic credit

Foreign liabilities/total liabilities

Year	All (percent)	T (percent)	N (percent)
1990	31.6	34.0	23.8
1991	32.9	36.5	23.7
1992	32.7	36.0	25.0
1993	36.0	39.3	29.3
1994	43.9	50.5	30.6
1995	46.4	53.5	34.2
1996	44.8	52.7	32.6
1997	47.4	54.8	37.2
1998	48.4	56.6	37.8
1999	44.9	52.1	36.4
2000	45.4	51.8	37.0
2001	44.4	52.1	35.6
2002	40.6	46.7	33.1

Note: Average of outstanding foreign currency liabilities over total liabilities.

the increase in the share of foreign-denominated debt from an average of 35 percent of the total in 1990–1994 to 45 percent during the credit crunch period (1996–2000; see table 6.11). Since the BMV set is biased toward the T sector, this contrast in financing opportunities explains why T-sector production did not fall so sharply in the wake of the crisis and why the GDP recovered so quickly.

Because the economic census does not provide data on the financing of firms, we look instead at the behavior of investment. We group the observations into quintiles and compute the change in the investment rate between 1994 and 1999.[7] Figure 6.4 shows that within each size class, the investment rate fell more in the N-sector firms than in the T-sector ones. Furthermore, the quintile that contains the largest T-sector firms is the only group that experienced an increase in the investment rate. Table 6.12, which reports the average investment rate across all size classes, shows that in 1994,

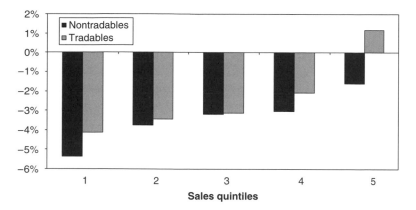

Figure 6.4
Change in the investment rate between 1994 and 1999
Notes: The investment rate is measured as net investment in fixed assets over the total level of fixed assets. Sales are the total revenues derived from own activity. The value displayed is the average investment rate in 1999 minus its value in 1994.

Table 6.12
Sectoral asymmetries in investment
(Investment rates)

	1994	1999
	Average	
N	7.1 percent	3.7 percent
T	6.9 percent	4.6 percent
N/T	1.03	0.81

Note: The investment rate is computed as the ratio of investment/capital$_{(t-1)}$.
Source: Own calculations with data from the Mexican economic census.

before the crisis, both sectors had essentially the same investment rate (about 7 percent). In contrast, in 1999 the investment rate of the N sector was almost 1 percent lower than that in the T sector (3.7 versus 4.6 percent, respectively).

To see whether the sectoral asymmetry we observe across the quintile of largest firms in figure 6.4 is associated with an asymmetry in financing opportunities, we run a standard cash flow regression similar to that used by Fazzari, Hubbard, and Petersen (1988). We regress the investment rate on the change in sales, on cash flow, and on cash flow interacted with a dummy that equals one for nonexporting firms during the years 1995–1997 or 1995–1998. Following Fazzari, Hubbard, and Petersen, we interpret a positive effect of cash flow on investment as an indication of financing constraints (the change in sales controls for investment opportunities). We estimate the regression including fixed effects and using a GLS estimator. The positive coefficient on the interaction dummy in table 6.13 implies that in the wake of the crisis, cash flow was a more important determinant of investment for nonexporters than exporters. This means that nonexporters were more credit constrained in the wake of the crisis. This effect is significant at the 5 percent level in the period 1995–1997, and at the 10 percent level in 1995–1998.

Table 6.13
Cash flow regressions

Dependent variable: Investment/capital$_{t-1}$		
	1	2
Cash flow$_t$/K$_{t-1}$	0.04***	0.02**
	(0.01)	(0.01)
d(sales)$_t$/K$_{t-1}$	0.05***	0.05***
	(0.00)	(0.00)
Cash flow$_t$/K$_{t-1}$ * D$_{crisis}$ * D$_{nonexporters}$	0.15***	0.05*
	(0.05)	(0.03)
Observations	1430	1592
Number of firms	328	338
R^2	0.195	0.194

Notes: D$_{crisis}$ = 1 for the years 1995–1997 in regression 1, and for the years 1995–1998 in regression 2. D$_{nonexporters}$ = 1 if the firm does not export. The regressions are estimated with fixed effects by GLS. They include year dummies, but they are not reported. Standard errors are given in parentheses; *denotes significance at the 10 percent level, **indicates significance at the 5 percent level, and ***denotes significance at the 1 percent level.

Currency Mismatch and Banks Exposure to the N Sector

Currency mismatch exists when liabilities are denominated in foreign currency, while the income streams that must service these debts are denominated in domestic currency. Currency mismatch has become an important issue in MICs because sudden real depreciations significantly increase the debt burden of a large group of agents, generating a meltdown of the banking system.

Unfortunately, there are no readily available indexes of currency mismatch, so the question arises as to how best to measure this concept. First of all, currency mismatch need not be a problem that affects the aggregate economy; it is a sectorial problem that mainly affects the N sector. It may well be the case that there is enough foreign currency available to service the debt. If N-sector debtors and the banks that lend to them have currency mismatch, however, then a real depreciation might generate a meltdown, unless the government can implement a redistribution from the T to the N sector on short notice. Clearly, these fiscal transfers are not feasible.[8]

Since banks in MICs are heavily exposed to the N sector, we can get a more precise indicator of currency mismatch by looking at the balance sheet of the banking system. Table 6.14 shows that on average, only about a third of bank lending goes to firms that can potentially be classified as belonging to the T sector. This indicates that the banking system is strongly exposed to the N sector.[9]

Banks' strong exposure to the N sector means we cannot determine the degree of currency mismatch by simply comparing the liabilities and the assets of the banking system. A bank can have 20 percent of its liabilities as well as 20 percent of its assets denominated in dollars; however, if all the loans are granted to the N sector, there is a de facto currency mismatch because there is insolvency risk. It may be even more misleading just to compare the denomination of deposits and loans, as these are only a subset, and a small subset at that, of the total balance sheet.[10]

Table 6.14
Bank lending by sector

	Assets	
	Loans to N^1	Loans to T^2
Argentina (1995)	67.1[3]	32.9
Chile (1985)	60.1	39.9
Korea (1997)	74.8[5]	25.1
Mexico (1995)	66.0	33.9
Peru (1996)	59.2	40.8
Thailand (1997)	66.5	34.5
Turkey (1993)	34.0[4]	66.0[4]

Notes: 1. The N sector includes construction, real estate business, infrastructure, services, personal consumption, commerce, wholesale and retail, housing, electricity-gas-water, restaurants, hotels, and transportation—all small. 2. The T sector includes mining, quarrying, industry, agriculture, forestry, the industrial sector, foreign entities, primary production, imports, and trade—all large. 3. Does not include consumption or housing credit. 4. Only consumption credit is N. 5. N is proxied by small firms, and T is proxied by large firms.
Source: See appendix. (pp. 175/6)

Our index of currency mismatch compares the share of foreign currency liabilities of the banking system to the share of loans that are covered by export income. We compute the latter ratio by multiplying the share of bank lending that goes to the T sector by the share of T-sector output that is actually exported. Column 3 in table 6.15 shows that exporting firms sell the majority of their output in the domestic market. Thus, they too must earmark a large share of domestic currency revenue for servicing foreign currency debt.

Our index of currency mismatch is reported in column 5 of table 6.15. The estimates range from 2.97 for Korea in 1997, to 4.34 for Mexico in 1995.[11] To see that currency mismatch is mostly a sectorial, not an aggregate, problem, compare table 6.15 with table 6.16. Notice that the foreign debt service-to-exports ratio is low in countries having a high currency mismatch index. A banking system where only 15 to 30 percent of dollar loans are covered by exports

Table 6.15
Share of foreign currency liabilities covered by income from exports

	Liabilities	Assets	Foreign currency coverage of assets		Currency mismatch
	A	B	C	D	E
	Percent of foreign currency liabilities	Loans to T	Export/ output	B*C	A/D, (lower bound[3])
Argentina (1995)	35.0	32.9	0.30	9.8	3.57
Chile (1983)	46.7	39.9[1]	0.28	11.2	4.17
Korea (1997)	17.9[2]	25.1	0.34	8.53	2.97
Mexico (1995)	33.4	33.9	0.23	7.7	4.34
Peru (1996)	73.0	59.2	0.34	20.1	3.62
Thailand (1997)	22.3	34.5	0.17	5.8	3.85
Turkey (1993)	47.0	66.0	0.24	15.84	2.97

Notes: 1. Data on loans in Chile are from 1985. 2. Foreign liabilities data in Korea are from 1993—thus the mismatch in 1997 must have been much larger. 3. The results are biased against finding our hypothesis of currency mismatch in several important ways: off–balance sheet items are not included, which are primarily in foreign currency; due to legislation, banks tend to underreport their foreign currency holdings as a share of liabilities (see Kamin and von Kleist (1999)); and we assume that all revenues from exports can be used to service the debt. All firms in potentially T sectors are assumed to indeed be T.
Source: See appendix. (pp. 175/6)

is certainly subject to substantial real exchange rate risk. This is true even though the aggregate measures of table 6.16 do not indicate currency mismatch.[12]

Systemic Bailout Guarantees

Despite the fact that bailout guarantees have played an important role in several explanations of boom-bust cycles, the evidence supporting the existence of this distortion is mainly anecdotal. Although many countries have systemic guarantees in place, it is

Table 6.16
Aggregate indicators of currency mismatch

	Foreign debt service/exports	Foreign debt/exports
Argentina	0.37	4.73
Chile	0.26	2.13
Korea	0.09	0.76
Mexico	0.36	2.30
Peru	0.25	5.77
Thailand	0.18	1.47
Turkey	0.56	3.60

Source: World Bank development indicators, 1994.

difficult to document the existence of such guarantees directly because, in most cases, they are implicit. To begin with, they are not limited to promises to hand bailout payments to lenders in case of default but are often implied in the exchange rate regime and monetary policy rules. Since in most instances one of the objectives of policymakers is to avoid sharp drops in output, they will implement policies that are, de facto, implicit guarantees against systemic crises.[13]

We investigate whether there are implicit guarantees by looking at the behavior of interest rate spreads. The idea is that if guarantees are present, the spread will, ceteris paribus, be insensitive to a deterioration in the average quality of loans (assuming, of course, that no crisis has yet occurred). When a crisis occurs, the quality of loans collapses and the spread skyrockets.

An ideal way to measure the evolution of the loans' quality is with the "true" share of nonperforming loans (NPLs). Unfortunately, such data in time-series form do not exist for most MICs. A good proxy for an increase in NPLs is the occurrence of a lending boom in the recent past. When there is a sharp acceleration in credit, the monitoring capacity of both banks and regulators is diminished, so that there is an increase in the likelihood of granting

Table 6.17
Implicit bailout guarantees

Dependent variable: Interest rate spread

	Panel A: Eight MICs		Panel B: All MICs	
	1	2	3	4
$LB_{j,t-1}$	2.559***	1.330	1.455***	0.205
	(0.930)	(0.875)	(0.448)	(0.519)
$D_{j,t} * LB_{j,t-1}$		3.849***		2.840
		(1.131)		(0.981)
Adjusted R^2	0.531	0.636	0.631	0.634
Number of observations	74	74	218	218

Notes: The table shows the estimates of the panel regression in (6.4). The lending boom dummy, LB, is equal to 1, if the growth rate of real credit has been larger than 10 percent on average for the past two years. The crisis dummy, D, indicates that a twin crisis occurred in t or $t+1$. The regressions are estimated with fixed effects, using a GLS estimator. Standard errors are reported in parentheses; *indicates significance at the 10 percent level, **indicates significance at the 5 percent level, and ***indicates significance at the 1 percent level.

credit to bad projects. The increase in the share of NPLs may take some time to materialize because it takes time for a given loan to become nonperforming, and because during the boom a lot of new loans are being granted. Nonetheless, after some time NPLs must become a problem for the banking system. This is true regardless of whether NPLs are officially recorded.

To capture this idea, we run the following panel regression:

$$i_{j,t} = \alpha_j + \beta_1 LB_{j,t-1} + \beta_2 D_{j,t} * LB_{j,t-1} + \varepsilon_{j,t}, \tag{6.4}$$

where $i_{j,t}$ is the real lending rate in country j at time t, minus the U.S. federal funds rate. $LB_{j,t-1}$ is a dummy that indicates the existence of a lending boom. It is equal to 1 if, during the past two years, real credit has grown by more than 10 percent on average. $D_{j,t}$ is a dummy variable that indicates that a twin crisis has occurred at t or $t-1$.

The coefficient a_1 measures the effect of an increase in NPLs on the spread in country years in which a crisis has not occurred in either the current or previous years. Meanwhile, the sum $\beta_1 + \beta_2$ measures the effect of an increase in NPLs on the spread during crisis times (at t or $t - 1$). As we discussed above, in order to isolate the effect of guarantees, we need to distinguish between periods in which a crisis has *not* occurred recently and periods in which a crisis *has* occurred recently. This is because systemic crises are typically preceded by lending booms, and during crises the spread shoots up.

The null hypothesis that there are systemic guarantees is $H(0)$: $\beta_1 = 0$. Table 6.17 shows the estimates of regression 1. Panel A considers a set of eight often-studied countries, and panel B considers all MICs. In both cases, we cannot reject the null at the 10 percent significance level. That is, we cannot reject the presence of implicit systemic guarantees. Interestingly, if the crisis dummy is disregarded and the interest rate is regressed only on the lending boom dummy, the estimated coefficient is statistically significant at the 10 percent level.

If we were to define systemic guarantees literally as promises to give bailout payments to lenders in case of default, we could investigate the proportion of crises that have triggered this type of bailout and then impose rational expectations to infer the ex ante implicit guarantee. Bordo and Schwartz (2001) along with Jeanne and Zettelmeyer (2001) find evidence of ex post bailouts during the last two decades and the early banking crises of the twentieth century.

7   Conclusions and Policy Implications

This book brings together two opposing views of financial liberalization. In one view, liberalization induces excessive risk taking, increases macroeconomic volatility, and leads to more frequent crises. In another view, it strengthens financial development and contributes to higher long-run growth. This book shows that these two views of liberalization are complementary.

The data reveal that in countries with severe credit market imperfections and functioning financial markets, financial liberalization leads to more rapid economic growth and financial deepening. This higher growth path is not a smooth process, however. Rather, it takes place through booms and busts. These boom-bust cycles exhibit many properties that are common across middle income countries (MICs) independently of the nominal exchange rate regime. We have also shown that the strong amplification of credit market shocks is not limited to crises times but is also evident during normal times.

In order to analyze macroeconomic patterns in MICs, it is not sufficient to look at aggregate data alone. Asymmetrical responses of the tradables (T) and nontradables (N) sectors are key to understanding the links among liberalization and growth, boom-bust cycles, and macroeconomic fluctuations more generally. Such asymmetries derive from the fact that in MICs, there are severe contract enforceability problems. Many T-sector firms are able to overcome these problems and gain access to international capital markets, whereas most N-sector firms are financially constrained and depend on domestic banks for their financing.

Trade liberalization promotes faster productivity growth in the T sector, but is of little direct help to the N sector. Financial liberalization adds even more to growth because it eases financing constraints, leading to an increase in investment by financially constrained firms, most of which are in the N sector. Nevertheless, the easing of financing constraints takes place through the undertaking of credit risk, which leads to financial fragility and occasional crises. Borrowers find it profitable to take on credit risk because there are systemic bailout guarantees that cover lenders against systemic defaults.

We conclude with a list of seven policy implications. First, although several observers have claimed that financial liberalization is not good for growth because of the crises associated with it, this is the wrong lesson to draw. The empirical analysis shows that across countries with functioning financial markets, financial liberalization leads to faster average long-run growth, even though it also leads to occasional crises. This gain in growth is over and above that derived from trade liberalization.

A second, closely related implication is that trade and financial liberalization will not solve the structural problems of a country. The first-best solution is to implement judicial reform and improve contract enforceability. In the absence of such reform, liberalization permits financially constrained firms to attain greater leverage and invest more, at the cost of undertaking credit risk. Credit risk creates an environment of rapid growth and financial fragility.

We agree with the general view that Foreign Direct Investment (FDI) is the safest form of capital inflow. The third implication, however, is that FDI does not obviate the need for risky international bank flows. FDI goes mostly to T-sector firms and financial institutions. As a result, bank flows are practically the only source of external finance for most N-sector firms. Curtailing such risky flows would reduce N-sector investment and generate bottlenecks that would limit long-run growth. Bank flows are hardly to be recommended, but for most firms it might be that or nothing. Clearly, allowing risky capital flows does not mean that anything goes. Appropriate prudential regulation must also be in place.

One is tempted to say that if a government had the appropriate information, the optimal policy would be to transfer resources to those in the population with better entrepreneurial skills and let them make the investing decisions. Of course, we now know that this is wishful thinking. After many failed experiments of this sort carried out during the last century, we now know that either governments do not possess the appropriate information, or crony capitalism and rampant corruption take over. A forth implication of our analysis is that since direct made-to-measure government transfers are not feasible, a second-best policy is to liberalize financial markets and allow banks to be the means through which resources are channeled to financially constrained firms—most of which are in the N sector. Here, it is key to make a distinction between "systemic" and "unconditional" bailout guarantees. The former are granted only if a critical mass of agents default. The latter are granted on an idiosyncratic basis, whenever there is an individual default. We have argued that if authorities can commit to only grant systemic guarantees, and if prudential regulation works efficiently, then financial liberalization will induce higher long-run growth in a credit-constrained economy. In contrast, if guarantees are granted on an unconditional basis or there is a lax regulatory framework, the monitoring and disciplinary role of banks will be negated. Therefore, financial liberalization will simply lead to overinvestment and corruption. We would like to emphasize that this book does not defend such lax policies.

The findings summarized in this book do not imply that crises are a good thing. They are nonetheless part of the growth process in financially liberalized countries with severe contract enforcement problems. The fifth implication is that there is no point in trying to delay an inevitable crisis. At the "tipping point," beyond which it is unlikely that capital outflows will reverse, authorities should focus on what to do after the crisis instead of attempting to forestall it with unsustainable policies. Delaying an inevitable crisis will tend to make the effects of the full-blown one far worse, as attested to by the experiences of Mexico in 1994 and Argentina in 2001.

Sixth, GDP growth typically recovers rapidly from a crisis. Sustainable long-run growth, however, cannot be assured unless the banking problem is fixed. Recovery in aggregate activity is typically not uniform across the economy. The T sector may grow strongly while the N sector recuperates only sluggishly. This asymmetrical response is intimately linked to a severe credit crunch that hits the N sector particularly hard and goes hand in hand with a steady increase in the share of nonperforming loans. The experience of the last two decades shows that nonperforming loans are unlikely to disappear on their own, even if GDP growth resumes quickly. This raises the question of whether a policy under which all nonperforming loans are recognized at once and the fiscal costs are all paid up front is preferable to a piecemeal policy. On the one hand, if they are recognized, the most likely outcome is that the government will have to take over the banking system, make a once-and-for-all bailout payment, and incur a huge fiscal cost up front. This will increase government debt and interest rates. On the other hand, if just a small share of nonperforming loans are recognized, the up-front bailout and fiscal cost will be low. Yet this strategy might generate perverse incentives and lead to evergreening—as the accrued interest on nonperforming loans is capitalized over and over again. Over time, the banking problem might grow and the credit crunch might last longer.

Seventh, one can draw a lesson for empirical implementation. Statistical variance is not a good instrument with which to identify financial fragility. The *fragility* in the context of our discussion is associated with infrequent but severe crises. While these infrequent crises lead to higher variance of macroeconomic variables, other frequently occurring disturbances, like bad economic policy or exogenous shocks, will also lead to higher variance. The variance of the distribution is therefore not sufficient to identify occasional crisis episodes in the data. By contrast, skewness, the third moment of the distribution, is able to discriminate between the two sources of variance. *Only if* crises are rare and of substantial size will the skewness of the credit growth rate be negative. Our argument has shown that infrequent crises are a by-product of a rapid-growth path. Hence, we view skewness as a better indicator for studying the effect of financial liberalization on economic growth.

Finally, we would like to point out that the above policy lessons are only applicable to the group of middle-income countries with functioning financial markets and severe contract enforceability problems. In particular, the argument supporting growth-enhancing credit risk does not apply to high-income countries where credit market imperfections are not severe.

Appendix: Data Sources and Definitions

Here, we describe how we construct our liberalization indexes and the N-to-T output ratio as well as the data sets we have used.

Liberalization Indexes

Our de facto trade and financial liberalization indexes signal the year when a given country has liberalized. We construct the indexes by looking for trend breaks in trade and financial flows. We identify trend breaks by applying the CUSUM test of Brown, Durbin, and Evans (1975) to the time trend of the data. This method tests for parameter stability based on the cumulative sum of the recursive residuals.[1]

An MIC is trade liberalized (TL) at year t if its trade-to-GDP ratio has a trend break at or before t, or the country's trade-to-GDP ratio has been larger than 30 percent at or before t. The 30 percent criterion identifies countries where trade was liberalized at the beginning of our sample (1980) or the increase in trade flows did not take place from one year to the next but over a few years.[2]

To determine the date of financial liberalization, we consider net cumulative capital inflows (CI).[3] A country is financially liberalized (FL) at year t if the KI has a trend break at or before t and there is at least one year with a KI-to-GDP ratio greater than 5 percent at or before t; or its KI-to-GDP ratio is greater than 10 percent at or before

t, or the country is associated with the European Union. The 5 and 10 percent thresholds reduce the possibility of false liberalization and false nonliberalization signals, respectively. Table A1 exhibits the liberalization dates.

In order to determine the trend breaks, we regress each KI series on a constant and a time trend. The test signals parameter instability of the time trend if the cumulative sum exits the area between the two critical lines. The test is based on the statistic: $W_t = \sum_{r=k+1}^{t} w_r/s$, for $t = k + 1, \ldots, T$, where w_r is the recursive residual and s is the standard error of the regression fitted to all T-sample points. If the coefficient on the time trend remains constant from period to period, $E(W_t) = 0$. But if it changes, W_t will tend to diverge from the 0 mean-value line. The significance of any departure from the 0 line is assessed by reference to a pair of 5 percent significance lines. The distance between them increases with t. The 5 percent significance lines are found by connecting the points $k \pm 0.948(T - k)^{1/2}$ and $T \pm 3 * 0.948(T - k)^{1/2}$. A crossing of the critical lines by W_t signals coefficient instability.[4]

When the cumulative sum of residuals starts to deviate from 0, it may take a few years until this deviation is statistically significant. In order to account for the delay problem, we choose the year where the cumulative sum of residuals deviates from 0, provided that it eventually crosses the 5 percent significance level. In the case of Mexico, parameter instability begins in the fourth quarter of 1989, and it becomes statistically significant after the fourth quarter of 1991.

Three comments are in order. First, our TL and FL indexes do not allow for policy reversals: once a country liberalizes it never becomes closed thereafter. This means that our indexes do not capture some policy reversals that might have occurred in the latter part of the 1990s. Since our sample period is 1980–1999, we consider that our approach is the correct one to analyze the effects of liberalization on long-run growth and financial fragility.[5] Second, in comparing different indexes it is convenient to distinguish *liberal-*

ization from *openness* indexes. The former identify *dates* of financial liberalization, while the latter measure the amount of capital flows that a country receives over a certain time period. For instance, Bekaert, Harvey, and Lundblad (2001), and Kaminsky and Schmukler (2002) consider liberalization indexes as we do, while Kraay (1998), Lane and Milesi-Ferretti (2002), and Edison et al. (2002) consider openness indexes. Finally, the country years identified as financially liberalized by our index as well as the other liberalization indexes do not coincide with "good times," as they include both boom and bust country years. Therefore, they are not subject to the criticism that liberalized country years coincide with good times. The liberalization dates are reported in table A1.

The N-to-T Output Ratio

We construct the N-to-T output ratio by proxying N-sector and T-sector production with data for construction, manufacturing, and services. In the main body of this book, we use the sectorial exports-to-GDP ratio as the criterion to select the N and T sectors. Construction is never classified as a T sector. Meanwhile, the classification of services and manufacturing varies from country to country. Since the price of N goods tracks international prices less closely than that of T goods, we construct an alternative index where we classify as N (T) the sector in which the sectorial real exchange rate varies the most (the least). Table A1 reports both indexes. The correlation between them is 0.745.

Mexican Manufacturing Sector Data Set

The data used to test for the presence of bottlenecks comes from the *Annual Industrial Survey (Encuesta Industrial Annual)* of the National Institute of Statistics, Geography, and Informatics. In 1999 the sample contained 5,934 firms, it covered more than 80 percent of manufacturing value added, 34.9 percent of employment, and

Table A1
Indexes

Country	Indicator of financial liberalization	Indicator of trade liberalization	N/T index based on export shares	N/T index based on real exchange rates
Argentina (ARG)	1991	1986	C/M	C/M
Belgium (BEL)	Always	Always	C/M	C/M
Bangladesh (BGD)	Never	Never	S/M	S/M
Brazil (BRA)	1992	1988	S/M	S/M
Chile (CHL)	Always	Always	C/M	C/M
Colombia (COL)	1991	1992	S/M	S/M
Egypt (EGY)	Always	1991	S/M	S/M
Spain (ESP)	Always	1984	S/M	S/M
Greece (GRC)	Always	1986	S/M	S/M
Hungary (HUN)	1994	1994	S/M	S/M
Hong Kong (HKG)	Always	Always	NA	NA
Indonesia (IDN)	1989	1987	S/M	S/M
India (IND)	Never	1994	S/M	S/M
Ireland (IRL)	Always	Always	NA	NA
Israel (ISR)	1990	1986	NA	NA
Jordan (JOR)	1989	Always	S/M	S/M
Korea (KOR)	1985	Always	C/M	C/M
Sri Lanka (LKA)	Never	1989	S/M	S/M
Morocco (MAR)	Never	1986	S/M	S/M
Mexico (MEX)	1989	1988	C/M	C/M
Malaysia (MYS)	Always	Always	C/M	C/M
Pakistan (PAK)	Never	Never	S/M	S/M
Peru (PER)	1992	1987	M/S	S/M
Philippines (PHL)	1989	1986	C/M	C/M
Poland (POL)	Never	1993	NA	S/M
Portugal (PRT)	1986	1986	C/M	C/M
South Africa (SOU)	1994	Never	S/M	S/M
Thailand (THA)	1988	1986	C/M	C/M
Tunisia (TUN)	Never	Always	M/S	S/M

Table A1
(continued)

Country	Indicator of financial liberalization	Indicator of trade liberalization	N/T index based on export shares	N/T index based on real exchange rates
Turkey (TUR)	Always	1994	C/S	C/M
Uruguay (URU)	1989	1988	NA	NA
Venezuela (VEN)	Never	Always	S/M	S/M
Zimbabwe (ZWE)	Never	Never	S/M	S/M

Notes: In the first two columns, "always" means that a country has been open at least since 1980, and "never" means that it was closed until 1999. In the third and fourth columns, C = construction, M = manufacturing, and S = services. For Indonesia, our sample does not cover the period before 1993. We therefore set 1989 as the liberalization date, which fits to the dates of Kaminsky and Schmuckler (2002) and Bekaert, Harvey, and Lundblad (2001).

83.6 percent of sales in the manufacturing sector. The unit of observation is the manufacturing establishment. For confidentiality reasons, however, we received the information at a five-digit aggregation level. To compute the share of N inputs, we consider the following as N expenses: maintenance and repair services, outsourcing services, rents and leasing, transport, publicity, and electricity. The other expenses used to calculate total variable costs include labor costs, materials, technology transfers, commissions for sales, combustibles, and other expenses.

Mexican Stock Market (BMV) Data Set

The data set is derived from the information contained in the financial statements of firms listed on the BMV. It is an unbalanced panel of 310 firms, excluding financial firms, of which only 64 are present for the whole sample period. We have yearly observations from 1990 to 2000. All the variables are measured at the end of the year and are deflated by the December Consumer Price Index. The variables used in the text are constructed as follows:

• Issuance—Total value of equity plus long-term bonds issued domestically and internationally. Long-term bonds are those with maturities of one year or longer. Issuances are normalized with the sum of long-term liabilities plus the stock outstanding.

• Entries/Listed Firms—Number of new firms or firms issuing Initial Public Offerings (IPOs) over total number of listed firms.

• Exits/Listed Firms—Number of firms de-listing over total number of listed firms.

• Foreign Liabilities/Total Liabilities—Liabilities denominated in foreign currency, over total liabilities.

• Capital Stock—Fixed assets, including real estate, machinery, and equipment.

• Investment—Change in fixed assets from year $t - 1$ to t.

• Cash Flow—Total sales minus operation expenses.

• Change in Sales—The change in total sales from year $t - 1$ to t.

Mexican Economic Census

The census covers the whole Mexican economy and is available at five-year intervals. The information at the establishment level is confidential. Thus, each observation corresponds to a group of establishments with a similar number of employees, the same economic activity (six-digit classification), and the same geographic region (municipality).[6] The number of establishments is omitted for some observations. In such cases, an average of the number of establishments by group is used in order to weight each. There were 286,866 observations in 1994, and 400,120 in 1999.

World Business Economic Survey **(WBES)**

The *WBES* was conducted by the World Bank in 1999. Variables included in the probit regressions were: label var gcf "General constraint—financing"\ 1 = no obstacle, 4 = major obstacle; label var exp_yn "Exports"\ 1 = yes, 2 = no; label var exp_pct % of output exported; label var yr_estb "year established"; and label var gvt_pct "Percent government ownership."

World Bank Development Indicators

The World Bank development indicators of the World Bank cover most variables in our sample of thirty-five MICs and seventeen HICs. Variables used in the boom-bust cycle as well as panel regressions include: Real GDP growth rates (code: NY.GDP.MKTP.KN); N/T: services (code: NV.SRV.TETC.KN), manufacturing (code: NV.IND.MANF.KN), interest rate spread (code: FR.INR.LNDP); real interest rate (code: FR.INR.RINR); gross domestic fixed investment (code: NE.GDI.FTOT.KN); and private consumption (code: NE.CON.PRVT.KN).

International Financial Statistics

From the international financial statistics of the International Monetary Fund, we used the following series: real exchange rate (lines ..RECZF); real credit growth: claims on private sector by deposit money banks (lines 22d..ZF), divided by the Consumer Price Index (lines 64..ZF); and deposits (demand deposits, lines 24..ZF + time, savings and foreign currency deposits, lines 25..ZF).

Other Sources

Organisation for Economic Cooperation and Development (OECD) Statistical Compendium, main indicators of industrial activity; Bank of Argentina; Bank of Brazil; Bank of Korea; Bank of Peru; Bank of Turkey; BANXICO; Direccion General de Investigacion Economica; Indicadores Economicos, May 1996 and 2001; Claudia

Dziobek, J. Kim Hobbs, and David Marston, "Toward a Framework for Systemic Liquidity Policy," IMF Working Paper 00/34 (Washington, DC: International Monetary Fund, 2000); Takatoshi Ito and Luiz A. Pereira da Silva, "The Credit Crunch in Thailand during the 1997–98 Crisis: Theoretical and Operational Issues with the JEXIM Survey"; Steven Kamin, Philip Turner, and Jozef Van't Dack, "The Transmission Mechanism of Monetary Policy in Emerging Market Economies: An Overview," Mimeo, Bank for International Settlements (BIS) conference; and OECD Bank Profitability statistics.

Notes

Chapter 2

1. In the United States, the effect of the spread on output has been considered an indicator that monetary shocks affect the economy through a credit channel, which is distinct from the traditional money channel.

2. The 1991 recession is often argued to have been characterized by a credit crunch in the United States.

Chapter 3

1. This chapter is based on Tornell, Westermann, and Martínez (2003).

2. The former group includes the G7 large industrial countries and those countries in which the rule-of-law index of Daniel Kaufmann, Aart Kraay and Pablo Zoido-Lobatón (1999) is greater than 1.4. A more exact term of the group would therefore be middle-enforceability countries rather than MICs. As the degree of contract enforceability measured in this index is highly correlated with the income level of the country, we refer to the set as HICs and MICs in the text for simplicity. The HICs are Australia, Austria, Canada, Denmark, Finland, France, Germany, Italy, Japan, Luxembourg, the Netherlands, New Zealand, Norway, Sweden, Switzerland, the United Kingdom, and the United States. The MICs are Argentina, Bangladesh, Belgium, Brazil, Chile, China, Colombia, Ecuador, Egypt, Greece, Hong Kong, Hungary, India, Indonesia, Ireland, Israel, Jordan, Korea, Malaysia, Mexico, Morocco, Pakistan, Peru, the Philippines, Poland, Portugal, South Africa, Spain, Sri Lanka, Thailand, Tunisia, Turkey, Uruguay, Venezuela, and Zimbabwe. The sample includes forty-one of the forty-four countries in the International Finance Corporation's emerging markets database, the exceptions being Costa Rica, Jamaica, and Singapore. Of these, the first two do not satisfy the 1 percent stock market turnover criterion, and for Singapore we do not have data.

3. Bekaert, Harvey, and Lundblad focus on stock market liberalization, which although highly correlated with financial and capital account liberalization, is distinct from both of these. Listed firms are a privileged set. Stock market liberalization gives them even more opportunities, but does not by itself relax the credit constraints on all other firms. Our argument is that financial liberalization promotes growth because it eases the borrowing constraints faced by the latter set of firms. Kaminsky and Schmukler's index of financial liberalization covers only a small subset of countries. Clearly, the definition of indexes and dummy variables influences the subsequent empirical results. The results do not qualitatively differ when using the related indexes mentioned above, however.

4. Granger causality test tests whether lagged values of one variable help to predict the values of another variable. The F-test tests the joint insignificance of all lagged variables.

5. Only one growth rate is shown for countries that were open or closed throughout the period. Country episodes of less than five years are excluded.

6. Exceptions are China, which performed better than predicted in spite of being closed, and Greece, which is an underperforming open economy.

7. Here an exception is Indonesia, which grew marginally less rapidly during the open period. Given Indonesia's major crisis in the postliberalization period, however, the fact that it recorded a growth rate above the predicted value in the second period is still remarkable. Note that even in cases (such as Brazil and the Philippines) where the growth rate is less than predicted, the gap between the actual and the predicted value is smaller during the open period.

8. Our panel is unbalanced because not all series are available for all periods. Our source of data is the World Development Indicators of the World Bank.

9. See, for instance, Bekaert, Harvey, and Lundblad (2001); Chari and Henry (2002); Dollar and Kraay (2002); Edison et al. (2002); Edwards (1998); Eichengreen (2001); Frankel and Romer (1999); Gourinchas and Jeanne (2003); Prasad et al. (2003); Quinn (1997); and Rodrik (1998).

10. On the link between lending booms and crises, see Gourinchas, Landerretche, and Valdes (2001); Kaminsky and Reinhart (1999); Sachs, Tornell, and Velasco (1996); and Tornell and Westermann (2002a). For a historical perspective, see Bordo and Eichengreen (2002).

11. During a lending boom, a country experiences positive growth rates that are above normal. These are not positive outliers, however, because the lending boom takes place for several years, and so most of the distribution is centered around a high mean. Only a positive one-period jump in credit would create a positive outlier in growth rates and generate positive skewness. For instance, the increase in capital inflows that takes place when a country liberalizes might generate such positive skewness.

12. The simplest nonparametric density estimate of a distribution of a series is the histogram. A histogram, however, is sensitive to the choice of origin and is not continuous. We therefore choose the more illustrative kernel density estimator, which smoothes the bumps in the histogram (see Silverman 1986). Smoothing is done by putting less weight on observations that are further from the point being evaluated. The kernel function by Epanechnikov is given by $(3/4)[1 - (\Delta B)^2]I(|\Delta B| \leq 1)$, where ΔB is the growth rate of real credit and I is an indicator function, which takes the value of 1 if $|\Delta B| \leq 1$ and 0 otherwise.

13. Skewness is computed over a ten-year period. Since the event window is based on only ten data points, we consider a shorter window.

14. Different definitions of the crisis dummy provide similar results. If we use, for instance, the banking crisis index of Von Hagen and Ho (2004), based on money market pressure for a sample of 47 countries, we find a value of 6 percent.

15. Although skewness measures shocks that happen only every ten years or less, it can still be measured in high-frequency data such as quarterly or annual growth rates. In these growth rate data, the "low-frequency" shocks also show up as outliers in the distribution.

16. Similarly, Veldkamp (2002) associates skewness with the incidence of asset price crashes.

17. Depending on the degree of autocorrelation in the shocks, it could be anything from one to infinity (the kurtosis of a normal distribution is equal to three).

18. In particular, among the MICs we consider during our sample period, there is no country that has experienced a major war that might have generated negative skewness in credit growth.

19. Since the higher moments of credit growth cannot be computed in a meaningful way when the observations are few, we consider only series for which we have at least ten years of data.

20. The overlapping-windows regression captures the spirit of the model we present below for the following reason. In the risky equilibrium of a liberalized economy, there is a probability $1 - u$ that a crisis will occur at time $t + 1$, given that a crisis does not occur at t. Meanwhile, in a nonliberalized economy, the probability of crisis is always 0. Therefore, according to the model, ten-year windows with more liberalized years should exhibit both greater negative skewness and more rapid growth than windows with fewer liberalized years.

21. The link between financial deepening and growth is well established in the literature. See, for instance, Demirgüc-Kunt and Levine (2001); and Levine, Loayza, and Beck (2000). See also the seminal work of McKinnon (1973).

22. Notice that the estimated coefficient on bumpiness is not capturing country fixed effects. Recall that, for each country, skewness varies over time, like all other variables, as we use ten-year rolling averages.

23. Ramey and Ramey (1995) and Fatas and Mihov (2002) show that fiscal policy–induced volatility is bad for economic growth.

24. Imbs's (2002) and Keisters and Ennis's (2003) results are consistent with this view.

25. The reason bumpiness enters with a positive sign in the fourth column is that all HICs are liberalized and have near zero skewness. Thus, negative skewness acts like a dummy that selects MICs that have liberalized financially.

26. We only highlight one specific example in this section. It may be viewed as a first step in a potentially interesting new research agenda for economic historians. We cannot claim at this point a definite conclusion about the link between bumpiness and growth in historical data. This is left for further research. For a more systematic discussion of historical crisis episodes, see Bordo and Eichengreen (2002).

Chapter 4

1. In the United States, the effect of the spread on output has been considered an indicator that monetary shocks affect the economy through a credit channel, which is distinct from the traditional money channel. See, for instance, Bernanke, Gertler, and Gilchrist (2000); Friedman and Kuttner (1992); and Stock and Watson (1989).

2. See Chinn and Kletzer (2000); Demirgüc-Kunt, Detragiache, and Gupta (2000); Eichengreen, Rose, and Wyplosz (1995); Frankel and Rose (1996); Gourinchas, Landerretche, and Valdes (2001); Gupta, Mishra, and Sahay (2001); Hutchison and Neuberger (2002); Kaminsky and Reinhart (1999); Krueger and Tornell (1999); Milesi-Ferretti and Razin (1998); Sachs, Tornell, and Velasco (1996); and Tornell (1999).

3. Banking Crisis (BC) and Currency Crisis (CC) dates are taken from Frankel and Rose (1996), Caprio and Klingbiel (1997) and Tornell (1999). A *joint crisis* is defined as an event where (1) BC and CC occur in the same year or in consecutive years; (2) in consecutive years, the year of the crisis is the year of the latter of the two; and (3) a joint crisis does not count if it occurs within three years before or after another joint crisis, or when a crisis occurs three or more years in a row.

4. In the latter case, we consider the earlier of the two the crisis date.

5. Event windows were constructed from panel regressions of the respective variable in each graph on dummy variables that take of value 1 in the period where a joint banking and currency crisis occurred and 0 otherwise. The panel regressions

are estimated with fixed effects using a GLS estimator. The N/T and GDP series were computed as midyear changes. The graphs are the visual representations of the point estimates and standard errors from the following pooled regression:

$$y_{it} = a_i + \sum_{j=-3}^{3} \beta_j Dummy_{\tau+j} + \varepsilon_{it},$$

where y is the respective variable of interest in the graph, $i = 1 \ldots 35$ denotes the country, $t = 1980 \ldots 1999$, and $Dummy_{\tau+j}$ equals 1 at time $\tau + j$ and 0 otherwise, where τ is a crisis time.

6. This and some of the other stylized facts, including credit to the GDP and the N/T output ration have meanwhile been replicated by Mendoza and Terrones (2004). Different views exist on how to better measure changes in the real exchange rate. Engel (1999) has argued that most of the variance in the real exchange rate is due to variations in the relative price of T at home and abroad. While this appears to be the case for the HICs he considers, in a study of fifty-two countries over the period 1980–2000, Betts and Kehoe (2001) find that variations in the real exchange rate reflect mainly changes in the relative price of N and T. In this book, we take the second view, and proxy the real exchange rate by the Producer Price Index (PPI)-to-Consumer Price Index (CPI) ratio.

7. An alternative explanation for the occurrence of banking crises is that there is a run on banks by depositors. Nevertheless, there is no evidence that during the last two decades, the problems faced by banks have been initiated by runs (see Demirgüç-Kunt, Detragiache, and Gupta [2000]).

8. See Jeanne and Zettelmeyer (2001).

9. Microlevel evidence on the asymmetrical financing opportunities of small and large (as well as T and N) firms will be presented in chapter 6.

10. The N sector is proxied by construction in ten countries, by services in eighteen countries, and by manufacturing in two countries. The T sector is manufacturing in twenty-seven cases and services in three cases. The results are robust to changes in the definition of N, such as definitions based on the variance of the sectoral real exchange rate, because for most countries both indicators coincide.

Evidence on the evolution of the N/T output ratio based on firm-level data is more difficult to obtain. Most surveys on N and T firms, such as the *World Business Economic Survey*, have data for only one year and do not allow us to trace the time path of output throughout a crisis. An exception is the World Bank's *Firm Analysis and Competitiveness Survey*. Hallward-Driemeier (2000) reports that exporters recover better after the crisis than do nonexporters. Other data sets, such as *Worldscope*, contain information about N and T firms in the time-series dimension, but include only large, stock-listed firms, and the patterns become more difficult to interpret in the context of our model. From our perspective, all of these firms would belong to the T sector. The evidence on large, stock-listed firms is mixed. Borensztein and Lee (2000) find that large *chaebol* firms do not have easier access to external finance than other stock-listed firms. On the other hand, they find that export-oriented firms experienced an increase in sales after the crisis. Using the *Worldscope* database, Forbes (2002) finds that in a set of forty-two countries, stock-listed firms with higher shares of foreign-sales exposure perform significantly better after depreciations.

11. The countries considered are Mexico (1994), Korea (1997), Thailand (1997), Sweden (1992), the Philippines (1997), Israel (1984), Malaysia (1997), Peru (1984), Finland (1991), and Brazil (1993). Although Sweden and Finland do not belong to our MIC set, we include them because they experienced well-known boom-bust episodes. For a discussion of the historical development of exchange rate regimes, see also Reinhart and Rogoff (2004). For a discussion of the link between exchange rate regimes and long-run growth, see also Razin and Rubinstein (2004).

12. The interpretation of these even windows is the same as in the previous section. The solid line traces the deviations from tranquil times. All variables are shown in levels.

13. The classification made by Reinhart and Rogoff (2004) is: Mexico, peg to U.S. dollar; Sweden, crawling peg around the DM; Thailand, peg to the U.S. dollar; the Philippines, peg to the U.S. dollar; Korea, crawling peg to the U.S. dollar; Israel, freely falling/managed floating; Peru, freely falling/freely floating; Malaysia, moving band around a basket of currencies; Finland, moving band around a basket of currencies; and Brazil, freely falling/freely floating. For a de jure classification of exchange rate regimes, see also Berger, de Haan, and Sturm (2000). A theoretical model of exchange rate regime choice is given in Berger, Jensen, and Schjelderup 2001.

14. This stylized fact is related to the equivalence of equilibriums under fixed and floating exchange rates established by Helpman (1981).

15. All variables are in first differences in order to avoid the issues associated with nonstationarity.

16. In MICs, T-sector firms have easy access to external finance because they can either pledge export receivables as collateral or can get guarantees from closely linked firms.

17. In chapter 5, we will explain why the interaction of financing constraints and systemic guarantees generates both currency mismatch and borrowing constraints.

18. The selection of countries is determined by the availability of quarterly data, in particular at the sectoral level. We have included countries for which we have at least seven years of quarterly data for all variables. Note that the length of the VAR

is not the same across countries. See the appendix for variable definitions and data sources.

19. In the literature for HICs, the ordering is not uncontroversial. For instance, Sims (1980) orders the interest rate in the first position of the VAR.

20. In 2002, Brazil exemplified this situation. The increase in the likelihood that a leftist candidate might win the presidential elections led to skyrocketing interest rates. The bailout program announced by the IMF in August, and the announcements of the incoming government, led to a reduction in the premium.

21. Note that although we do not report standard errors, the responses of the group of eight MICs are statistically highly significant. As we have an average of eight countries, the standard errors of the individual countries would have to be divided by $\sqrt{8}$ to evaluate the significance level. Thus, even if the point estimates were smaller than the standard errors individually, the grouped impulse responses would still be significant.
   As an alternative, we could have included dummies to capture an increase in the spread due to a crisis. If we were to do so, the main results would not change. Although the effect during crisis times is stronger, the total cumulative effect is only a bit smaller if the dummy is included (23 percent, in the case of Mexico).

22. This VAR is derived by assuming that N output is predetermined in a given quarter.

23. We have focused on real variables. Gali and Monacelli (2002) analyze monetary policy in a small open economy with price rigidities.

24. There is also a growing number of country studies that try to uncover the importance of credit market imperfections in MICs. See, for instance, Agenor, Aizenman, and Hofmaister (1998) for Argentina; Ber, Blass and Yosha (2002) for Israel; and Gelos and Werner (2002) for Mexico.

25. Related arguments about the difficulty of conducting monetary policy in the presence of severe credit constraints are discussed in Marin (2000).

Chapter 5

1. In chapter 6, we document the existence of the credit market imperfections we have described here.

2. The model combines elements of the financial accelerator framework (Bernanke, Gertler, and Gilchrist [2000]) with elements of third-generation balance-of-payments crisis models. See, for instance, Aghion, Bachetta, and Banerjee (2000); Burnside, Eichenbaum, and Rebelo (2000); Caballero and Krishnamurthy (1999); Calvo (1998); Chang and Velasco (1998); Corsetti, Pesenti, and Roubin (1999); Krugman (1999); McKinnon and Pill (1997); Mendoza (2001); and Tirole (2002).

3. Since the economy is small and open, the destination of T goods is not important for our argument.

4. Betts and Kehoe (2002) find that in a set of fifty-two countries over the period 1980–2000, real exchange rate variations reflect mainly changes in the relative price of N and T goods, not movements in the international relative prices of T goods. Among some developed countries, the latter channel is more important (Engel [1999]).

5. We can think of N firms as banks that lend to the N sector. This captures the fact that in MICs, banks are heavily exposed to the N sector. The banking system is the channel through which capital inflows reach the N sector, and is also the weak link during crises.

6. Recall the distinction between unconditional and systemic guarantees we made earlier. If all debts were covered by unconditional bailout guarantees, then the enforceability problem would become irrelevant and borrowing constraints would not arise in equilibrium.

7. Here, we do not analyze how the cost of the subsidy implicit in the guarantees is paid for. This cost could be financed by domestic taxation if we assumed that T goods were produced using a fixed factor. In this case, the cost of the subsidy would be paid for by taxing this fixed factor. This is done by Ranciere, Tornell, and Westermann (2003).

8. There are multiple self-fulfilling equilibriums, as in Cole and Kehoe (2000) and Obstfeld (1986).

9. Clearly, in the real world, financial liberalization opens up the possibility for agents to take on credit risk in many other ways than by simply allowing them to choose a risky debt instrument. Here, we capture this in a parsimonious way that allows us to obtain closed-form solutions, which in turn allows us to make clear why in an economy with credit market imperfections, financial liberalization leads to higher growth only if it leads to fragility.

10. For a derivation of this result, see Schneider and Tornell (2004).

11. The mechanism by which higher growth in the N sector induces higher growth in the T sector is the decline in the relative price of N goods that takes place in a growing economy $p_{t+1}/p_t = [\theta\phi^s]^{\alpha-1}$. If there were technological progress in the T sector, there would be a Balassa-Samuelson effect and the real exchange rate would appreciate over time.

12. We have set a_t to a constant. It can be verified that an increase in a_t following trade liberalization reduces N/T.

13. For a survey, see Bernanke, Gertler, and Gilchrist (2000).

Chapter 6

1. In MICs, T-sector firms have easy access to external finance because they can either pledge export receivables as collateral or get guarantees from closely linked firms. The existence of overall severe credit constraints is also supported by the importance of barter trade in transition economies, as documented and theoretically modeled by Marin and Schnitzer (1995).

2. Argentina, Brazil, Chile, the Czech Republic, Ecuador, Egypt, Estonia, Hungary, Indonesia, Lithuania, Mexico, Malaysia, Peru, the Philippines, Poland, Portugal, Russia, Slovakia, Slovenia, South Africa, Spain, Thailand, Turkey, Tunisia, Uruguay, and Venezuela. Schiffer and Weder (2001) describe this database in detail. The database is available from the World Bank at ⟨http://www.worldbank.org/beext/resources/assess-wbessurvey-alt.htm⟩.

3. We use the same approach as Schiffer and Weder (2001), who compare small and large firms with respect to financing constraints as well as other indicators of governance. They find that small firms are more constrained.

4. Buch et al. (2005) investigate a new firm level data set from Germany on FDI that is broken down by Size and by Sectors. They find that FDI mostly goes to the large tradable firms. Furthermore, they show that trade is overall a significant determinant of FDI, but in the construction sector, the only significant determinants are Common Border, EU Membership, and GDP. Being an MIC even significantly reduces the chances to obtain FDI in the construction sector.

5. Mexico liberalized its financial markets in 1989. In 1994 it experienced a major banking and currency crisis, known as the Tequila crisis. For more information about the process of liberalization, see Dornbusch and Werner (1994), Esquivel and Tornell (1995) and Babatz and Conesa (1997). For an analysis of the crisis in the spirit of this book, see Tornell and Krüger (1998) and Martinez and Werner (2002).

6. New equity issues are typically placed in New York through American depository rights.

7. Because of confidentiality requirements, each observation represents not a single firm but a group of firms. Each group contains firms that are similar in size, in the same subsector, and located in the same geographic area.

8. For papers that deal with currency mismatch, see Aguiar (2000); Arteta (2002); and Eichengreen, Hausmann, and Panizza (2003).

9. In order to bias the results against the hypothesis that banks are heavily exposed to the N sector, we assume that all firms in sectors that are commonly considered T are indeed T. Thus, we group manufacturing, mining, agriculture, forestry, and primary production as T, while construction, services, and electricity-gas-water are

considered N. Note that the fraction of bank lending that goes to consumption or housing credit is not covered by foreign currency income and thus also counts as N. In most countries, the figures would be even higher if these items were included (consumption and housing credit are available only for Hungary, Mexico, and Thailand).

10. For instance, foreign currency deposits in Thailand account for less than 10 percent of the total foreign external liabilities of the banking system.

11. Our estimates of currency mismatch are conservative. More realistic or accurate estimates would take into account that the amount of foreign currency revenue available to service debt is less than total foreign currency income. Some of the foreign currency income is required to pay off the factors of production.

12. A high foreign debt service-to-exports ratio signals a currency mismatch problem. Although this aggregate measure may be low, however, one cannot infer that there is no currency mismatch.

13. Systemic guarantees are not the same as deposit insurance schemes, which cover individual agents against idiosyncratic risk.

Appendix

1. All HICs have been trade and financially liberalized through our sample period.

2. We compute the trade-to-GDP ratio as the ratio of exports plus imports over the GDP. We use the *World Development Indicators* of the World Bank.

3. We compute net cumulative capital inflows of nonresidents since 1980. Capital inflows include FDI, portfolio flows, and bank flows. The data series are from the International Financial Statistics (IFS): lines 78BUDZF, 78BGDZF, and 78BEDZ. For some countries, not all three series are available for all years. In this case, we use the inflows to the banking system only, which is available for all country years.

4. The underlying assumption is that the time series is trend stationary before the structural break. This is confirmed for the case in Mexico by the following unit root tests:

Augmented Dickey-Fuller test statistic	T-statistic	P-value
1982:1–1989:4	−4.43	0.007
1982:1–1995:4	−2.33	0.409

The unit root tests are estimated with a constant, a time trend, and a number of lags (two) determined by the Schwartz Information Criterion (SIC) criterion. Before liberalization, the series is trend stationary. Including the postliberalization period, it has a unit root and is difference stationary.

5. If after liberalization a country suffers a sharp reversal in capital flows (like in a financial crisis), it might exhibit a second break point. In our sample, however, this possibility is not present: the trend breaks due to crises are never large enough to show up in significant CUSUM test statistics.

6. Within each six-digit class and each municipality, establishments were grouped according to the following stratification: 0–2 employees, 3–5, 6–10, 11–15, 16–20, 21–30, 31–50, 51–100, 101–250, 251–500, 501–1,000, and 1,001 or more.

References

Agenor, P., J. Aizenman, and A. Hofmaister. 1998. "Contagion, Bank Lending Spreads and Output Fluctuations." NBER Working Paper No. 6850. Cambridge, MA.

Aghion, P., P. Bachetta, and A. Banerjee. 2000. "Capital Markets and the Instability of Open Economies." Mimeo, Study Center Gerzensee, Switzerland.

Aguiar, M. 2000. "Foreign Currency Debt in Emerging Markets." Mimeo. University of Chicago.

Arteta, C. 2002. "Dollarization of Banking, Financial Stability, and Financial Liberalization." PhD diss., University of California, Berkeley.

Babatz, G., and A. Conesa. 1997. "The Effect of Financial Liberalization on the Capital Structure and Investment Decisions of Firms: Evidence from Mexican Panel Data." PhD diss., Harvard University.

Bekaert, G., C. Harvey, and R. Lundblad. 2001. "Does Financial Liberalization Spur Growth?" NBER Working Paper No. 8245. Cambridge, MA.

Ber, H., A. Blass, and O. Yosha. 2002. "Monetary Policy in an Open Economy: The Differential Impact of Exporting and Non-Exporting Firms." Mimeo, Tel Aviv University.

Berger, H., J. de Haan, and J. E. Sturm. 2000. "An Empirical Investigation into Exchange Rate Regime Choice and Exchange Rate Volatility." CESifo Working Paper No. 263. Munich.

Berger, H., H. Jensen, and G. Schjelderup. 2001. "To Peg or Not to Peg? A Simple Model of Exchange Rate Regime Choice in Small Economies." *Economics Letters* 73, no. 2:161–167.

Bernanke, B. 1990. "On the Predictive Power of Interest Rate Spreads." *New England Economic Review* (Nov.–Dec.):51–68.

Bernanke, B., and M. Gertler. 1989. "Agency Costs, Collateral and Business Fluctuations." *American Economic Review* 79:14–31.

Bernanke, B., M. Gertler, and S. Gilchrist. 2000. "The Financial Accelerator in a Quantitative Business Cycle Framework." In *Handbook of Macroeconomics*, ed. P. Taylor and M. Woodford. Amsterdam: Elsevier North-Holland.

Betts, C., and T. Kehoe. 2001. "Real Exchange Rate Movements and the Relative Price of Nontraded Goods." Staff Report. Federal Reserve Bank of Minneapolis.

Borchardt, K. 1982. *Wachstum, Krisen, Handlungsspielräume der Wirtschaftspolitik.* Göttingen: Vandenhoeck and Ruprecht.

Bordo, M., and B. Eichengreen. 2002. "Crises Now and Then: What Lessons from the Last Era of Financial Globalization." NBER Working Paper No. 8716. Cambridge, MA.

Bordo, M., and A. Schwartz. 2001. "Measuring Real Economic Effects of Bailouts." NBER Working Paper No. 7701. Cambridge, MA.

Borensztein, E., and J.-W. Lee. 2000. "Financial Crisis and Credit Crunch in Korea: Evidence from Firm-Level Data." IMF Working Paper No. 25. Washington, DC.

Brown, R. L., J. Durbin, and J. M. Evans. 1975. "Techniques for Testing the Constancy of Regression Relationships over Time." *Journal of the Royal Statistical Society* 37:149–192.

Buch, C., J. Kleinert, A. Lipponer, and F. Toubal. 2005 (in press). "Determinants and Effects of Foreign Direct Investment: Evidence from German Firm-Level Data." *Economic Policy.*

Burnside, C., M. Eichenbaum, and S. Rebelo. 2001. "Prospective Deficits and the Asian Currency Crisis." *Journal of Political Economy* 109:1155–1197.

Caballero, R., and A. Krishnamurthy. 1999. "International and Domestic Collateral Constraints in a Model of Emerging Market Crises." *Journal of Monetary Economics* 48:513–548.

Calvo, G. 1998. "Capital Flows and Capital Market Crises: The Simple Economics of Sudden Stops." *Journal of Applied Economics* 1, no. 1:35–54.

Caprio, G., and D. Klingbiel. 1997. "Bank Insolvency: Bad Luck, Bad Policy, or Bad Banking." In *Annual World Bank Conference on Developing Economics*, ed. M. Bruno and B. Plaskovic. Washington, DC: World Bank.

Chang, R., and A. Velasco. 1998. "Financial Crises in Emerging Markets: A Canonical Model." NBER Working Paper No. 6606. Cambridge, MA.

Chari, A., and P. Henry. 2002. "Capital Account Liberalization: Allocative Efficiency or Animal Spirits?" NBER Working Paper No. 8908. Cambridge, MA.

Cheung, Y.-W., and K. S. Lai. 1993. "Finite Sample Sizes of Johansen's Likelihood Ratio Tests for Cointegration." *Oxford Bulletin of Economics and Statistics* 55:313–328.

Chinn, M. D., and K. M. Kletzer. 2000. "International Capital Inflows, Domestic Financial Intermediation, and Financial Crises under Imperfect Information." NBER Working Paper No. 7902. Cambridge, MA.

Cole, H., and T. Kehoe. 2000. "Self-Fulfilling Debt Crises." *Review of Economic Studies* 67:91–116.

Corsetti, G., P. Pesenti, and N. Roubini. 1999. "Paper Tigers: A Model of the Asian Crisis." *European Economic Review* 43:1211–1236.

Demirgüç-Kunt, A., E. Detragiache, and P. Gupta. 2000. "Inside the Crisis: An Empirical Analysis of a Banking System in Distress." IMF Working Paper No. 00/156. Washington, DC.

Demirgüç-Kunt, A., and R. Levine. 2001. *Financial Structure and Economic Growth: A Cross-Country Comparison of Banks, Markets, and Development.* Cambridge, MA: MIT Press.

Diamond, D., and R. Rajan. 2000. "Banks, Short-Term Debt, and Financial Crises." NBER Working Paper No. 7764. Cambridge, MA.

Dollar, D., and A. Kraay. 2002. "Institutions, Trade, and Growth." Carnegie Rochester Conference Series on Public Policy.

Dornbusch, R., and A. Werner. 1994. "Mexico: Stabilization, Reform, and No Growth." Brookings Papers on Economic Activity, 253 297.

Edison, H. J., R. Levine, L. Ricci, and T. Slok. 2002. "International Financial Integration and Growth." *Journal of International Money and Finance* 21:749–776.

Edwards, S. 1998. "Capital Flows, Real Exchange Rates, and Capital Controls: Some Latin American Experiences." NBER Working Paper No. 6000. Cambridge, MA.

Eichengreen, B. 2001. "Capital Account Liberalization: What Do Cross-Country Studies Tell Us?" University of California, Berkeley.

Eichengreen, B., R. Hausmann, and U. Panizza. 2003. "Currency Mismatches, Debt Intolerance, and Original Sin: Why They Are Not the Same and Why It Matters." NBER Working Paper No. 10036. Cambridge, MA.

Eichengreen, B., A. Rose, and C. Wyplosz. 1995. "Exchange Market Mayhem: The Antecedents and Aftermath of Speculative Attacks." *Economic Policy* 21(October):249–312.

Engel, C. 1999. "Accounting for U.S. Real Exchange Rates." *Journal of Political Economy* 107, no. 3:507–538.

Esquivel, G., and A. Tornell. 1995. "The Political Economy of Mexico's Entry into NAFTA." In *The annual East Asian NBER Conference*, ed. T. Ito and A. Krueger.

Fatas, A., and I. Mihov. 2002. "The Case for Restricting Fiscal Policy Discretion." CEPR Discussion Paper No. 3277. Washington, DC.

Fazzari, S. M., R. G. Hubbard, and B. C. Petersen. 1988. "Financing Constraints and Corporate Investment." *Brookings Papers on Economic Activity* 1:141–195.

Forbes, K. J. 2002. "How Do Large Depreciations Affect Firm Performance?" Unpublished Paper. Department of Economics, MIT, Cambridge, MA.

Frankel, J. A., and D. Romer. 1999. "Does Trade Cause Growth?" *American Economic Review* 89, no. 3:379–399.

Frankel, J. A., and A. K. Rose. 1996. "Currency Crashes in Emerging Markets: An Empirical Treatment." *Journal of International Economics* 41, no. 3:351–366.

Friedman, B. M., and K. N. Kuttner. 1993. "Economic Activity and the Short-Term Credit Markets: An Analysis of Prices and Quantities." *Brookings Papers on Economic Activity* 2.

Friedman, B. M., and K. N. Kuttner. 1998. "Indicator Properties of the Paper-Bill Spread: Lessons from Recent Experiences." *Review of Economics and Statistics* 80:34–44.

Gali, J., and T. Monacelli. 2002. "Monetary Policy and Exchange Rate Volatility in a Small Open Economy." NBER Working Paper No. 8905. Cambridge, MA.

Gelos, G., and A. Werner. 2002. "Financial Liberalization, Credit Constraints, and Collateral: Investment in the Mexican Manufacturing Sector." *Journal of Development Economics* 67, no. 1:1–27.

Gertler, M., and S. Gilchrist. 1994. "Monetary Policy, Business Cycles, and the Behavior of Small Manufacturing Firms." *Quarterly Journal of Economics* 109:309–340.

Gourinchas, P. O., and O. Jeanne. 2003. "The Elusive Gains from International Financial Integration." NBER Working Paper No. 9684. Cambridge, MA.

Gourinchas, P. O., O. Landerretche, and R. Valdes. 2001. "Lending Booms: Latin America and the World." NBER Working Paper No. 8249. Cambridge, MA.

Gupta, P., D. Mishra, and R. Sahay. 2001. "Ouput Response to Currency Crises." Paper presented at the second annual IMF Research Conference, Washington, DC, November 29–30.

Hallward-Driemeier, M. 2000. "Firm-Level Survey Provides Data on Asia's Corporate Crisis and Recovery." Unpublished Paper. World Bank, Washington, DC.

Helpman, E. 1981. "An Exploration in the Theory of Exchange Rate Regimes." *Journal of Political Economy* 89:865–890.

Hoffmann, W. G. 1965. *Das Wachstum der Deutschen Wirtschaft seit der Mitte des 19 Jahrhunderts.* Berlin: Springer.

Holmstrom, B., and J. Tirole. 1997. "Financial Intermediation, Loanable Funds, and the Real Sector." *The Quarterly Journal of Economics* 112:663–691.

Hutchison, M. M., and I. Neuberger. 2002. "How Bad Are Twin Crisis? Output Cost of Currency and Banking Crisis." Unpublished Paper. Department of Economics, University of California, Santa Cruz.

Imbs, J. 2002. "Why the Link between Volatility and Growth Is Both Positive and Negative." Mimeo, London School of Economics.

Jeanne, O., and J. Zettelmeyer. 2001. "International Bailouts, Moral Hazard, and Conditionality." *Economic Policy* 33(October):409–432.

Kamin, S. B., and K. von Kleist. 1999. "The Evolution and Determinants of Emerging Markets Credit Spreads in the 1990s." Bank for International Settlements Working Paper No. 68. Basel, Switzerland.

Kaminsky, G., and C. Reinhart. 1999. "The Twin Crises: The Causes of Banking and Balance of Payments Problems." *American Economic Review* 89:473–500.

Kaminsky, G., and S. Schmukler. 2002. "Short-Run Pain, Long-Run Gain: The Effects of Financial Liberalization." World Bank Working Paper No. 2912. Washington, DC.

Kashyap, A., and J. Stein. 2000. "What Do a Million Observations on Banks Say about the Transmission of Monetary Policy?" *American Economic Review* 90, no. 3:407–428.

Kashyap, A., J. Stein, and D. Wilcox. 1993. "Monetary Policy and Credit Conditions: Evidence from the Composition of External Finance." *American Economic Review* 83, no. 1:78–98.

Kaufmann, D., A. Kraay, and P. Zoido-Lobatón. 1999. "Governance Matters." World Bank Policy Research Working Paper No. 2196. Washington, DC.

Keisters, T., and H. Ennis. 2003. "Economic Growth, Liquidity, and Bank Runs." *Journal of Economic Theory* 109:220–245.

Kiyotaki, N., and J. Moore. 1997. "Credit Cycles." *Journal of Political Economy* 105, no. 2:211–248.

Konrad, K. A. 1992. *Risikoproduktivität: Contemporary Studies in Economics.* Heidelberg, Berlin: Springer.

Kraay, A. 1998. "In Search of Macroeconomic Effects of Capital Account Liberalizations." Mimeo, The World Bank, Washington, DC.

Krueger, A., and A. Tornell. 1999. "The Role of Bank Restructuring in Recovering from Crisis: Mexico 1995–1998." NBER Working Paper No. 7042. Cambridge, MA.

Krugman, P. 1999. "Balance Sheets, the Transfer Problem, and Financial Crises." Mimeo, MIT, Cambridge, MA.

Lane, P., and G. Milesi-Ferretti. 2002. "The External Wealth of Nations." *Journal of International Economics* 55, no. 2:263–294.

La Porta, R., F. Lopez de Silanes, and G. Zamarripa. 2002. "Related Lending." NBER Working Paper No. 8848. Cambridge, MA.

Levine, D., N. Loayza, and T. Beck. 2000. "Financial Intermediation and Growth: Causality and Causes." *Journal of Monetary Economics* 46, no. 1:31–77.

Levy-Yeyati, E., and F. Sturzenegger. 2000. "Classifying Exchange Rate Regimes: Deeds vs. Words." Mimeo, IMF, Washington, DC.

Marin, D. 2000. "Monetary Policy Does Not Work in Russia's Barter Economy—German Banking as a Solution?" *Economic Systems* 24, no. 1:87–90.

Marin, D., and M. Schnitzer. 1995. "Tying Trade Flows: A Theory of Countertrade with Evidence." *American Economic Review* 85, no. 5:1047–1064.

Martínez, L., and A. Werner. 2002. "The Exchange Rate Regime and the Currency Composition of Corporate Debt: The Mexican Experience." *Journal of Development Economics* 69:315–334.

McKinnon, R. 1973. *Money and Capital in Economic Development.* Washington, DC: Brookings Institution.

McKinnon, R., and H. Pill. 1997. "Credible Economic Liberalizations and Overborrowing." *American Economic Review* 87, no. 2:189–193.

McKinnon, R., and H. Pill. 1999. "Exchange-Rate Regimes for Emerging Markets: Moral Hazard and International Overborrowing." *Oxford Review of Economic Policy* 15:19–38.

Mendoza, E. 2001. "Credit, Prices, and Crashes: Business Cycles with a Sudden Stop." NBER Working Paper No. 8338. Cambridge, MA.

Mendoza, E., and M. Terrones. 2004. "Are Credit Booms in Emerging Markets a Concern?" IMF World Economic Outlook Conference, Washington, DC.

Milesi-Ferretti, G., and A. Razin. 1998. "Current Account Reversals and Currency Crisis: Empirical Regularities." NBER Working Paper No. 6620. Cambridge, MA.

Newey, W., and K. West. 1987. "A Simple, Positive, Semi-Definite Heteroskedasticity and Autocorrelation Consistent Covariance Matrix." *Econometrica* 55:703–708.

Obstfeld, M. 1986. "Rational and Self-Fulfilling Balance of Payments Crises." *American Economic Review* 76:72–81.

Prasad, E., K. Rogoff, S. Wei, and A. Kose. 2003. "Effect of Financial Globalization on Developing Countries: Some Empirical Evidence." Washington, DC: International Monetary Fund.

Quinn, D., 1997. "The Correlates of Change in International Financial Regulation." *American Political Science Review* 91(September):531–551.

Rajan, R., and L. Zingales. 1998. "Financial Dependence and Growth." *American Economic Review* 88:559–586.

Ramey, G., and V. Ramey. 1995. "Cross-Country Evidence on the Link between Volatility and Growth." *American Economic Review* 85, no. 5:1138–1151.

Ramey, V. 1993. "How Important Is the Credit Channel in Monetary Transmission?" *Carnegie-Rochester Conference Series on Public Policy* 39:1–45.

Ranciere, R., A. Tornell, and F. Westermann. 2003. "Growth and Crises: A Re-evaluation." NBER Working Paper No. 10073. Cambridge, MA.

Razin, A., and Y. Rubinstein. 2004. "Growth Effects of the Exchange-Rate Regime and the Capital-Account Openness in a Crises-Prone World Market: A Nuanced View." Mimeo. University of Tel Aviv.

Reinhart, C. M., and K. S. Rogoff. 2004. "The Modern History of Exchange Rate Arrangements: A Reinterpretation." *Quarterly Journal of Economics* 119, no. 1(February):1–48.

Rodrik, D. 1998. "Who Needs Capital-Account Convertibility." Harvard University, Cambridge, MA.

Sachs, J., A. Tornell, and A. Velasco. 1996. "Financial Crises in Emerging Markets: The Lessons from 1995." Brookings Papers on Economic Activity, 147–198.

Sachs, J. D., and A. M. Warner. 1997. "Fundamental Sources of Long-Run Growth." *American Economic Review* 87, no. 2(May):184–188.

Schiffer, M., and B. Weder. 2001. "Firm Size and the Business Environment: Worldwide Survey Results." International Finance Corporation Discussion Paper 43. Washington, DC.

Schneider, M., and A. Tornell. 2004. "Balance Sheet Effects, Bailout Guarantees, and Financial Crises." *Review of Economic Studies* 71, no. 3:883–913.

Silverman, B. W. 1986. *Density Estimation for Statistics and Data Analysis*. London: Chapman and Hall.

Sims, Chris. 1980. "Macroeconomics and Reality." *Econometrica* 48:1–48.

Sinn, H.-W. 1986. "Risiko als Produktionsfaktor." *Jahrbücher für Nationalökonomie and Statistik* 201:557–571.

Stock, J. H., and M. W. Watson. 1989. "Interpreting the Evidence on Money-Income Causation." *Journal of Econometrics* 40, no. 1:161–182.

Tirole, J. 2002. *Financial Crises, Liquidity, and the International Monetary System*. Princeton, NJ: Princeton University Press.

Tornell, A. 1999. "Common Fundamentals in the Tequila and Asian Crises." NBER Working Paper No. 7193. Cambridge, MA.

Tornell, A., and A. Velasco. 1992. "The Tragedy of the Commons and Economic Growth: Why Does Capital Flow from Poor to Rich Countries?" *Journal of Political Economy* 100, no. 6:1208–1231.

Tornell, A., and F. Westermann. 2002a. "Boom-Bust Cycles: Facts and Explanation." *IMF Staff Papers* 41:111–165.

Tornell, A., and F. Westermann. 2002b. "The Credit Channel in Middle Income Countries." NBER Working Paper No. 9355. Cambridge, MA.

Tornell, A., F. Westermann, and L. Martinez. 2003. "Liberalization, Growth, and Financial Crisis: Lessons from Mexico and the Developing World." *Brookings Papers on Economic Activity* 2:1–112.

Veldkamp, L. 2002. "Slow Boom, Sudden Crash." Mimeo. INSEAD.

Von Hagen, J., and T. Ho. 2004. "Money Market Pressure and the Determinants of Banking Crises." ZEI Working Paper No. B20, Rheinische Friedrich-Wilhelms University, Bonn.

Zamagni, V. 1993. *The Economic History of Italy: 1860–1990*. Oxford: Clarendon Press.

Abbreviations

FDI	Foreign direct investment
HICs	High-income countries
LICs	Low-income countries
MICs	Middle-income countries
N-sector	Nontradables sector
N/T	Nontradables-to-Tradables output ratio
T-sector	Tradables sector

Index